To Ly
Best
L

...arley

Footsteps without Prints

To Best Wishes
Ceri Pugh

To Lynette,
Hope you enjoy the book as much as we enjoyed writing it. Rhian.

To lynette
enjoy the artwork
Dennis.

What comes to mind is walking along the beach one day with such difficulty. As I am walking my feet sink into the sand, even though the sand seems solid. What is most surprising is walking along the beach a week later at the same point, and this time no footprints left. The sand is solid. This is most puzzling. I share these thoughts with others, though I am told the sand is wet. Thinking back, the beach seems the same, though something *is* different.

Footprints, Alan Bowen

Footsteps without Prints

Edited by
Lenni Charles
Alan Bowen
& Nyfed Griffiths

ICONAU

Published by Iconau
Fernbank
Ferryside
SA17 5SR
www.iconau.com

First published in 2009

ISBN 978-1-905762-94-1

Edited by Lenni Charles, Alan Bowen & Nyfed Griffiths

Front cover image © Denise Searl
Back cover image © Rhain F. Miles

Design & typesetting by Lucy Llewellyn
www.lucyllew.com

Printed and bound by Dinefwr Press, Llandybïe, Wales

Carmarthenshire Mental Health Forum

British Library Cataloguing in Publication Data

A cataloguing record for this book is available from the British Library.

Contents

Foreword

My summer journeys from Pontardawe to Hafal in Carmarthen in 2008 seemed always to be sunny. This was not due to the weather, but because I was on my way to work with an intelligent, aware, and articulate group of writers. When our course ended I hoped that I had given some inspiration and guidance in support of their wish to publish their own work.

Here is the proof that their commitment has resulted in success. Here is pleasure, pain, wit and sincerity. Writing is often difficult, but the feeling of liberation and confidence gained in expressing yourself in words is well worth the effort.

I wish *Footsteps without Prints* all the acclaim it deserves.

With fond memories,

Carole Morgan Hopkin M.A.

Footsteps without Prints

Haiku

Nyfed Griffiths

Here is a Haiku written about the form of Haiku.

Condensed expression;

An effectual impact,

Capturing Essence.

Sticky Times

Rhian F. Miles

Once upon a time, there was a stick insect that was Janeen's favourite pet, and it lived with her in a glass case in her bedroom. Her mum and dad were all too happy with this, because Janeen spent all her time locked away in her room with her pet. Mr Stick had a habit of spitting out a 'sticky' substance (when Janeen picked him up) and he would 'stick' like glue to her clothing... I think it was his way of showing that he loved her! Janeen would love to tie pieces of string to his legs, and hang him from curtain poles, because when the blinds were open and the sun shone through, he became luminous and it was a beautiful sight! Sometimes Janeen could not see him in the same light, because he shone so bright he almost blinded her.

One day, she grabbed some string and took him out of the case into the garden. She didn't want him to escape, so she tied him to the apple tree in the orchards at the back. Whilst there, she spotted a piece of bark from the tree, and it had several rings about it (showing its age). She picked a single ring up, and proceeded to place it on the insect's forearm – Mr Stick was alarmed, but Janeen persevered until the deed was done. Then she held Mr Stick and chanted a medieval song she had learned many years ago, which she believed united her with the one she loved, and Mr Stick became a 'branch' of the family.

For hours, Jan and Mr Stick had fun out in the sunny orchard. Jan ate pears, apples, blackcurrants and gooseberries until she was fair full up. Mr Stick, too, ate leaves on the branch until his tummy was fair full, and he stuck out like a sore (Tom) thumb on the tree! But the two of them were happy as Larry, playing in the midday sun, they stuck around for a while, until the sun closed down, and Mr Stick was no longer luminous and Janeen could see to cut him down from the branch. Mr Stick was having so much fun, he wanted Jan to 'stick' around for a while longer, and when she picked him off the tree, he 'stuck' out his tongue and spat out his glue onto her thumb, uniting them completely.

For many more memorable years, Mr Stick and Janeen lived happily together, playing in the sunshine in the garden, with 'sticky' stuck to her thumb. It was a friendship and love that was destined forever, where no one could tear them apart, in their very secret world!

The Letter

Lenni Charles

Dear Roy,

I do not know where you are or even if you are still alive; neither do I expect your forgiveness, only that you try to understand.

When I said I wanted to end our relationship and you asked me if it was because of your colour, I said yes. I lied. Or I lied in as much as only by association. I have never had any problems with colour as such. My best friend at school was Afro-American and my ex-partner was an African prince, therein lies the rub! I suffered such dreadful abuse at the hands of his family, friends and himself that twice I nearly died and I ended up having twin sons who died minutes after being born. My friends thought I would not survive, but after some eighteen months in a psychiatric hospital I was deemed fit to go out into the world.

I was at art school in Rochester but half way through the second year I had a breakdown and had to drop out. After that I worked at the Royal Photographic Society for a couple of years, good wages, my own secretary, but I became bored and depressed. I worked as a nanny for a while and then found a job in a pub, which was when I met you.

I looked at you across the bar and fell into your lovely brown eyes. I did not believe that anyone so beautiful could find me attractive but after a few days you asked me out and I was over the moon. Very quickly our friendship grew and we became lovers, so when you asked me to meet your mother and your family, my response should have been one of delight, instead of which I panicked. For six months, we had lived in our little bubble, our safe cocoon, and now I had to face the world, your world. Again I had to enter another culture, maybe more friendly than Sam's. I did not know. Some would accept us, some would be more hostile. Was I strong enough to do this again and, more important, was I strong enough to do it and at the same time not hurt you or ruin our relationship with the shadows of the past. My very state of panic seemed to answer this question and so I decided that I was too damaged to be good for you and must end our love before too much hurt was done. It was the hardest thing that I have ever had to do, to watch you walk away, shoulders slumped and dejected. I longed to call you back, try to explain, hold you in my arms, feel safe, but it would have been selfish to ask you to take on the emotional cripple that I was then.

The med I fled to was a loud mouthed, psychotic gangster, someone I knew I could neither love nor trust but whom I would have to keep my wits about me with, if you don't let your guard down you can get hurt.

That was all a long time ago and in the last thirty odd years I have had three long term partners, all of them neither whole or wholesome. The first two were alcoholics and third was a drug addict. Not that I haven't had a lot of fun at times, but I had this feeling that I really had dreadful taste in men. I think now though with hindsight that I picked out men who were weaker than me so that I was always the one in control so I couldn't get hurt.

About ten years ago, whilst on a counselling course I found that I had not as I had thought always hated the sight and smell of roses but that it went back to the time when I had just lost the twins and was lying in this tiny hospital room with a high temperature and sweat running down my arms and everyone had bought me roses, bunches and bunches. Then the registrar got me to sign a book to say that the twins were still-born. They were not but it would save them the price of a funeral. I think that was the point at which I stopped caring.

I live on my own now with just my ginger cat and apart from those six months with you I'm as happy as I have ever been in my life. I hope you soon forgot me and found someone who made you happy and who you enjoyed your life with. I have two lovely daughters and four grandchildren, the youngest of who stayed with me last week; whilst she was here I had a strange dream. I dreamt that I had been divorced and that my ex-husband had come back and asked that we go for counselling in order to get back together. I had not made up my mind about it but was considering it.... when I woke up feeling very happy. The funny thing was that when I thought about it I didn't recognise the man as any of my ex-partners. Then I remembered Jung saying that the people we dream about are not other people but different parts of ourselves, so the healing is still going on.

I still think of you sometimes and wonder what would have happened if I had followed my heart. The heart regrets but the mind still believes it was the sensible thing at the time.

Maybe someday when we die we will meet again in heaven where souls have no colour or creed and it is safe to love.

Correspondence with a Mouse

Nyfed Griffiths

Dear Mousie,

I'm leaving you this letter. Don't eat it. Read it!

If you want to reply, I've left a small pen and some paper for you.

Whether you're Mickey or Minnie – I've tried to put all the food away in boxes or containers, so you can't reach it or nibble at it with your little sharp teeth. The trouble is with you, that when you eat food, you adulterate it and you leave it unfit for us humans to eat, or we might catch some disease. I don't know what you think. Any comment Mousie?

I feel I should apologise, since I'm corresponding with you, that I've tried to catch you in a trap. Isn't that horrendous for you, Mousie? I realise you have your own life to lead, but I'd rather not have my food dirtied by you. If my name was Rhian, I'd have a sad ending to this tale. (Rhian was a member of the Creative Writing class.) How's *your* tail?

I hand over to you, now, Mousie.

Nyfed.

Dear Nyfed,

Well, I like your kitchen, Nyfed. It's nice to look for whatever crumbs I may find in it, though that isn't usually much.

So, I'm glad you haven't caught me in your trap, or that would be the end of me. You're right. Yes, I have a life to lead!

I think I'll be back again, on the scrounge, but I'll steer clear of the trap. So, thanks for your communication, Nyfed. Ciao!

Respectfully yours ('Respectfully' because you deemed me worthy to communicate with),

Mousie, as you call me, though my name is actually Miranda – Miranda Mouse, or to give me my full name in mousie circles – Miranda 'cheese and chocolate' Mouse, because I've got a nose for both and a liking for both.

Enough now! Yours, Miranda.

To my precious daughter Carrie on the death of a friend

Rhian F. Miles

I write to you with a heavy heart, regarding the death of an old friend 'Mars-behind-bars', who died in his bed in the early hours of the morning. He followed my route to this planet in his 'souped-up-super-spacecraft' many years ago and we became firm friends from that day! He used to house his spaceship in his dilapidated shed at the bottom of the garden, where it was recharged every night, and during the day we would travel the world in it, watching skies changing from azure blue to midnight black; snow-capped mountains melting to display browns and copious green crags; and seas ebbing and flowing in an ever-changing tide in front of our own eyes. They were such wonderful times, and memories spring forth of a sincere friendship that was so dear to me.

'Mars-behind-bars' didn't have many friends because he had a goldfish bowl as a face and he looked different from other humans. He wore the glass bowl over his head to recharge the oxygen in his lungs, and it also housed several goldfish swimming around; when he got hungry, he would open his mouth and swallow them one at a time! He had the unique ability to regurgitate the fish, and once brought back from his gut, they turned out to be solid gold. After he regurgitated them, little children would spot golden objects lying on the ground and pick them up as golden pebbles or nuggets and take them home to their mums and dads to show their treasures. When the parents saw them they were enchanted and immediately set to work making coronets out of cardboard to house the golden fish then place on their children's heads as coronation crowns. This was indeed the 'Golden Age' when every child was a golden prince or princess and the mums and dads were pearly kings and queens.

But when all is said and done, 'Mars-behind-bars' was truly a golden friend and he left his legacy behind by departing with a glorious fishy ending and how the fish got away! And now Rita (the writer) was left without her dear friend – no more space hopping and travelling faster than the speed of sound; and all that was left was the darkest final goodbye, accompanied by a lasting lament. The greatest of friends must never say goodbye. And one day soon, we'll gather rainbows up on high!

With fondest love,

Rita

Going to the Theatre

Anonymous

On thinking of the theatre, one cannot escape the name of William Shakespeare the bard.

Thinking about some proposition fairly recently, Bassanio's speech in 'The Merchant of Venice' inescapably came to mind: 'The world is still deceived with ornament. In Law, what plea so twisted and corrupt but, being season'd with a gracious voice obscures the show of evil? In religion, What damn'd error but some sober brow will bless it and approve it with a text hiding the grossness with fair ornament?' (Act III Sc ii)

Mind you, the reason I referred to either the bard or his particular work is entirely the result of some 'blood, sweat and tears' shed for my WJEC 'O' level in English Literature, it being a set book. I have set it as one of my objectives in life to see this play being performed. I think that it came as a touring company some years ago either to Kidwelly or Pembroke or both but as an open air show.

The only play of note that I can remember was in Swansea's Grand Theatre, a modernised version of Euripides' profound 'Women of Troy' as perfectly performed as in Greece, Ephesus or Aspendos and in a different vein Agatha Christie's 'Murder @ the vicarage' ably performed by the multi-talented Ruth Madoc and Ruby Murray transformed into Miss Marples.

Roll back the years as a child seeing 'Reluctant Heroes' performed @ the Prince of Wales Theatre Cardiff which has since disappeared. I suppose I've arrived at a time of life when I can perceive the advantage of theatre over the contemporary media of cinema and television.

Such presentations as the dramatisations of William Golding's 'Lord of the Flies' was another example of utilising modern technology to enhance dramatic effects, as was 'Wind in the Willows' in Carmarthen.

The appearance of cinema and television certainly hasn't heralded the end of theatre thank goodness.

A Description (See, Observe, Remember)

Nyfed Griffiths

It's a medium-sized room – large enough to move around in – though not as large as a room for a wedding reception. It's a bit cold in winter months, so when we have meetings then, we put both electric heaters on. The storage heaters lose their heat over the day, so in winter evenings they don't make much difference.

We have to be thankful of course. It's not as if we live in that cold a climate, like Siberia or the Arctic, where the Eskimos used to live. It would be freezing inside their igloos, even though there might be a baby there. The Eskimos rubbed seal fat or would it be whale blubber on their bodies to keep themselves warm.

Back to the room. It's bright and airy with white coloured walls and vertical blinds for privacy or to block out glare, which would make it difficult to see what's on a laptop screen, because of reflection. There are four reasonably sized rectangular tables, pushed together in the room, making plenty of space to spread out work. There is also ample seating for people in a meeting, but if necessary more chairs can be brought in from another room.

The staff who look after the place are friendly and helpful, with a kind and welcoming boss. The staff are very accommodating and this helps in the efficient running of the place. The rooms are used by several organisations. I know of about six or seven, and am directly involved in four of the organisations which use the rooms.

Today, I'm at one of my favourite activities – creative writing – and this is a creative writing exercise. These sessions have been running for well over six months and I feel it has been and is a successful venture. It has been arranged by WWAMH – West Wales Action for Mental Health – and ArtsCare/GofalCelf have arranged the tutors and laptops and digital cameras for the course. I am typing this out on one of the laptops.

A goal of this activity is to produce a book of all our creative work – written work of different natures, photography and art work, like cartoons, for example. The deadline for the book has been postponed, but I hope momentum won't be lost because of this.

This is a positive and constructive venture in which ArtsCare/GofalCelf, WWAMH and ourselves, the service users, are involved. I see creative writing and speaking as an immensely valuable form of self-expression. It helps in a person's self-fulfilment and developing of potential as an individual, in my opinion. So, as the Scots say, if I've got the spelling right: 'Long may your lang reek', or in other words long may it continue.

A Poem

S. Lewis

When I was born I wasn't wanted,
So I went into foster care.
Here I was tried and tested.
I suffered abuse and rape, pain and loss,
And it was all too much to bear.
At 14 I managed to tell a bit.
Just to escape – I felt in despair.
No one knew how much I hurt,
I felt they never listened to my words.
So I turned to self abuse – self harm it's called.
I often took it too far,
And I began to try and end my life,
So this began chapter 2 of a life called pain.
I was placed on section at the premature age of 15,
I was often medicated and restrained,
And I was called by some *insane*,
I got moved around so many different hospitals

For my safety could never be maintained.
'Post Traumatic Stress Disorder' –
My first diagnoses.
'Take this tablet' I got told.
'It'll make you feel better – take the pain away'.
'And talk to us; tell us it all – it always helps to share'.
So new tablet after new tablet I took –
Nothing made a difference.
And I couldn't talk – because if they knew,
They just really wouldn't care.
So my life turned into a blur,
I was intent on bringing it to an end.
But no suicide attempt I made ever worked,
And I ended up in more pain.
Broken legs, dialysis, operations –
I couldn't do this any more.
'You're suffering from BPD –
But we're afraid there is no cure –
You will grow out of it in your 30s'.
So 15 more years of pain to go,
How could I survive that long?
'Oh and we're afraid no medication will help you.'
So I decided the self harm must carry on.
But nobody understood me and everyone started to reject me.
I had become my own worst enemy.
And I knew I had to try to change.

So at the age of 26, I made a choice –
I had to get out there in the world.
But I knew it wasn't going to be easy,
As for my whole life I had been contained,
But I fought through each day,
In the hope that one day I would wake up free from pain.

So I stopped all the self harming
And trying to end my life;
Each day things got a little easier,
And as I started to change,
People around me began to change.
I was respected more for trying to cope,
My words were finally being heard.
I found that people wanted to help now –
Instead of having a duty to help.
Things are still not easy,
And no, I'm still not cured.
But I'm not even 27 yet,
So I know there's still plenty of time and years ahead.

The past I know I'll never forget,
But the self abuse has stopped –
I've turned it around to self respect.
Now chapter 3 has started and who knows where life will lead.
But now my thoughts are positive and I know I can succeed

Thumbs Up

Rhian F. Miles

Once upon a time, there was a young girl called Rita-Grita. She lived in the south of the island, and she kept a wonderful secret... she could make magic. Rita-Grita was only twelve years old when she learnt that she had this wonderful talent that only she could do... she could make inanimate things disappear; never to return!

She loved her family and friends with a passion but there was only the old man for her and she truly, truly adored him with all her heart. One day the old man was sitting on a rickety old stile next to his house and he beckoned Rita-Grita to him. He explained that many years ago he had given up the 'weed', and that never a day goes by without him wishing to 'light up' just once for old time's sake! Rita-Grita took pity on him and quickly ran away to her bedroom. In the room, she opened up her ballerina musical box where she kept all her treasures and there, for sure, were two golden coins. She slipped out of the house, waving gaily to the old man; and ran right along the country lane (which was one mile in length) to the village shop.

'Hello Rita-Grita,' said the shopkeeper, 'what can I do for you young lady?'

'My old man wishes for some top class weed that he denied himself some forty years; and I know he would be over the moon if he had just one!'

'Well dear... what about some Tom Thumb cigars... They're not cheap – have you got the money to pay?'

'Yes,' said Rita-Grita as she placed the golden coins in the shopkeeper's hand – and with that she was gone.

When she returned to the stile, the old was still there pontificating.

'Here you are old man,' she said. 'I know you secretly long for a puff, and I'm going to tell you my magic! Here is a tin of Tom Thumb cigars – and this is where I do my disappearing act. I will leave them with you and I will come back in 24 hours; and I'll hedge a bet that in that time, they'll have all disappeared!'

The Desk

Nyfed Griffiths

It was something I read in a feng shui book or something relating to feng shui and clutter that planted the seed in my mind. I thought I should have a desk in my lounge as a focal point as I do a lot of written work in the lounge, and I had such a desk in an upstairs room. I would need someone else's help to bring it down though.

One evening, I set about preparing. I cleared stuff away from around and on top of the desk, ready for ease of removal from the upstairs room. I also cleared a large space in the lounge downstairs, to manoeuvre and position the desk. It was to be up against the mantlepiece and fireplace. First I had to move a table that then occupied this place where the desk was to go. With some difficulty I managed this and put the table, which I discovered to have woodworm, in the junk room.

It was now time to ask a neighbour for some help, but first I thought I'd move the desk to the doorway of the upstairs room. By lifting one end at a time and swinging and dragging it round, I accomplished this. No way could I have bodily lifted the desk myself or I would have done myself an injury. But there are ways to get round this, which I was to further discover soon.

Having got to the doorway, I thought I'd try and get it through the door, before asking a neighbour for help. By aligning it up with the opening, sliding myself along the top of the desk, until I was through the doorway, and dragging it through, I accomplished this again. Now it was time to get a neighbour to help me get it down the stairs.

The desk was on the upstairs landing and I thought, 'Why can't I get it down to the mid-stairs landing by sliding it down on its top?' I tilted it over onto its top, which was flat, and going in front of it to control its speed, I slid it down the top flight of stairs with ease. I tilted it up on its end and walked it corner by corner over to the top of the second flight of stairs – the main flight.

I got in front of it and keeled it over so that I was supporting the leading end. By dragging it horizontally more or less forwards, it came down the stairs bump, bump as I retreated down – until I got down to the ground floor and lowered my end of the desk to the floor.

I then tilted the desk on its end and walked it over corner by corner to the lounge entrance. It was a pretty sturdy desk to take this treatment; I had bought it about thirty years ago, and the stairs had a carpet on them, so the desk didn't get marked. I lowered it down on to its feet by the entrance to the lounge and by dragging and lifting one end at a time got it through the doorway into the lounge. By further manoeuvring I got it into the position I wanted it and even succeeded in putting 'shoes' on the inner feet, which rested on the tiles in front of the fireplace. The outer feet rested on the carpet, which was at a higher level than the tiles; hence the need for 'shoes' under the inner feet to make the desktop level.

Of course, I hasten to add, I had removed all the drawers and contents of the desk to make it lighter, but it was still quite heavy and a bit cumbersome to move, but I had done it and without any help. I felt a sense of achievement that through trying, initiative and ingenuity I had succeeded in doing what I thought was impossible without help. There is a saying which is a comfort to me and goes like this:

'He who knows when to submit to fate and when to resist it, is its true conqueror.'

Now the desk is a focal point in my lounge and I've even succeeded in sealing the board over the fireplace with packing tape to keep out draughts from the chimney. I am well satisfied. Now for the next challenge!

The Mirror Room

Oskar Dremny

The man I had decided to study was not unusual in any way, not an intellectual, scientist or wit like my friends and me, but rather a normal man, one without ambition, who had consumed his way through life and therefore did not stand out from the consumerist mob. In fact, he blended in with a type of culture; a culture that had reeked of decadence in the final days of its existence; he reminded me of a late Roman, drunk with power and decadence, and as such he resembled the dark ages of a fallen empire.

Regardless of his social status, I have decided to focus on him as a candidate for observation; of course, as I am a clinical scientist my observations must be properly recorded and for that purpose I shall use some of the most up to date film equipment. It will allow me to consider with at least some impartiality why and how this man conducts himself within the confines of his own dangerously out of control culture.

The room has been prepared ready and I am truly excited to ascertain with some clarity, at least one aims for such things, an insight into the true horror of our own time – binge drinking. The mob; those that are ruled by concerns with sex, money and celebrity; these people are addicted to a world of consumption. No longer does debauchery reside in the affluent upper classes now it has transcended class and stature and is causing devastation amongst the middle, lower and under classes: alcohol transcends every attempt to curtail the beastliness that it unleashes on the world. Could it be that the world relishes a lack of clarity, meaning and hope and prefers a wine soaked perspective? Only my research can clarify what is happening, I trust I shall find something unique, something extraordinary… something to clarify what is happening.

As an observer of humanity, I fear that we face a great abyss that threatens to overwhelm us, and yet, did not the Romans fear just the same? It cannot pass that we will allow the mistakes of the past to slip past us unlearnt and unheeded; yet that and more, very much more, has already been forgotten. And that folly is now unheeded, it is amongst us like a foul beast that gorges itself from the swimming pool of alcohol it finds amongst us; in our houses, in our dreams, and our nightmares; it follows us, unremitting, unavoidable and undeniable.

I am conscious that I am digressing from my observations. The room is prepared and I have a clean notebook ready for any points of interest that seem worth some further investigation and analysis. Tonight I expect him to arrive whilst I am out. This was arranged to preserve his anonymity. It is essential that he is honest in his answers to my questions and therefore he does not have to reveal his identity unless he so wishes.

It is an arrangement for privacy and I CANNOT digress from that path; even though I long to stay and observe. Now, of course, you see my reliance on the cameras I have set up, a reliance that stems yet again from my own culture, as we are surrounded by the damn things. They are everywhere. The irony is that the cameras observe everything, the fights, the tears, the knives, the blood, yet the cameras don't comment or learn anything at all from what they see. They are blind; blinded from the fact that they see all and yet learn nothing; blind cameras watching the blind mob consume themselves in a world of alcohol-fuelled fear of each other. It is sad. We are the mere pawns in a chess game between sanity and madness and already we are short of a knight and a castle. The queen is safe but oh so old that we can no longer rely on her swift defence of the elongated straits of our culture.

And so back to the room; it is prepared and ready for the subject. I have left a series of intellectual questions that I hope will test the subject. I must go as I am late for a dinner with some friends. Being social and inquisitive is very important during these trying times, and in order to gain a sense of perspective I must endeavour to keep up appearances if nothing else.

Alas, I have overslept. I did thoroughly enjoy myself last night though. It was most invigorating. Although I completely missed the subject and his visit to the room, I didn't return till late last night after thoroughly enjoying myself at dinner. I would bore you with the details but the meal was rather excellent.

I have just checked the tapes in the room and found them all full with material. I can only assume that the candidate left when the tape finished. I made myself a coffee and then settled down to go over the recordings. I needed to find out what had been said during my absence so I rewound the tape quickly and quietly; after all, this was what I had been waiting for. There was no time to waste. I am sure that I have made adequate preparations for every eventuality, after all a scientist must try and be objective. I anticipate that the film will be most revealing about human nature.

I sipped my coffee, and hoped fervently that it would sooth the headache that seemed to have started when I awoke this morning. Curious about what awaited me, I played the tape.

Did I realise that pressing that button would release the beast inside the tape; not at that time, how could

I? I was naïve; full of my own importance, yet blissfully unaware of my own folly. Could I have foreseen it? I doubt it. How could I... but I digress... and indeed perhaps a small part of me did understand. The beast is subjective and hence so must I be. I am the observer. After all, that is the job of the scientist, to observe. I took a deep breath and pressed play.

I will never forget the voice. Its haunts me and yet its words define me. But as a scientist I must only report, observe, and then with empirical reticence rationalize what I have seen. In this process I have faith. I believe that it can make a difference.

The man, I do not even know his name such was the randomness with which the subject was selected, began to speak.

It was a harsh London accent, beastlike, unknowable and deeply repugnant to me. I listened in horror but I must write down what it said. Pray, do not be offended as I only offer this as evidence for my research. If only I knew his name, so that I could berate him in the cold light of day but, of course, it was impossible: for all intents and purposes, he may as well not exist, for it was impossible to find him.

Thus I leave you with his words: pray do not judge the scientist, he only observes the savage...

A large loud rather deep voice begins to speak,

'She's gagging for it. Look at her... she is you know!'

The tape recorder that I had placed in the room weeks earlier reacted to the sound of a human voice and then began to interact with a computer; the computer booted up a program that began to ask a set of predetermined questions. A cold clinical voice spoke out from the speaker that I had wired into the computer mainframe:

'WHO'

The man's response is immediate.

'The woman in the bar... the one in the small pink dress, with her legs showing...'

I couldn't bring myself to write that word, so I scrubbed it out, but I had to continue listening to this voice, it was unlike any voice I had ever heard. I was totally disturbed by the anger and fear that lay behind the words. The voice suddenly bellowed across the room:

'I COULD TASTE HER, SMELL HER, TOUCH HER. I NEEDED HER.... THOSE DOE-LIKE EYES... CONSUME HER. UNTIL THERE WAS NOTHING LEFT.'

The man paused, suddenly breathless from his explosion of misogynistic language. I was horrified. What had I done? Who was this monster I had unleashed? Why had I given him an audience? Already, I loathed him completely. He was nothing but a savage, an uneducated reprobate long since established in my own society. Why did I need and want to listen to this monster ranting? He was a creature without reason, yet instinctively on some human level, I must confess that undeniably and even ashamedly I was hooked by this outburst of savagery. I awaited the next question with anticipation.

'WHY'

The voice snarled in response.

'Why... who cares about why. Why is not important. Don't you understand? I'm hammered... hammered I tell you! Drunk, sloshed, pie eyed, kaput, legless. The why is not important! Why denotes a motive, an ulterior meaning that is somehow due to cause or effect. Tosh! The world is drunk on a meaningless drunken binge. WHY ask WHY? FOOL! Don't you drink? Don't you know? That is the point, imbecile. That is the reason that WHY has no relevance. Why did I drink until I fell, until I passed out in a gutter, in an attempt to confirm my own impure existence?

WHY, why what? It's those questions that have relentlessly driven us here. What do you mean you may ask. I will tell you but only as I'm DRUNK, so drunk that I can't see, or feel, or touch, but that is the point is it not? I am drunk as a skunk, kippered, plastered and any other way you want to name it. But I shall return to the point. FEAR, it drives us, consumes us, alienates us, betrays us, and if it is not fear then pure unrelenting anxiety. Anxiety of everything, terrorism, godlessness, religion; everything! For the sake of sanity, these questions are pointless, why does not exist. Get it over with.'

The man I observed was becoming increasingly agitated and hard to understand. I could not understand his ramblings but kept recording them for future research. I would have to spend many hours poring over the data to try and figure out what was at the centre of the beast's existence. I did not know why he was increasingly aggressive and I feared that I lacked the skills to deal with such a complicated case, but for the sake of science I knew that I must persevere. The computer was oblivious to the contradictions within the room and all too soon another question was being asked by its metallic emotionless mouth.

'WHEN'

The man grew increasingly angry. I still could not see his face but I could sense it as he began muttering in a series of unconnected words that meant little if indeed anything at all. I could not join the words together to find any meaning amongst these mutterings and for once I felt some anxiety of my own. Could I really understand this man who had sat in my research room last night? It seemed an almost impossible task. The man began to bang his head on the table in front of him. Hard, then harder, until finally the table began to jump off the floor with the impact of his head, and blood began to fly from his brow as his head jerked away from the table after impact. Finally, after many minutes, he stopped. He was quiet for a moment, and then he began to whisper, in an altogether quiet voice:

'The fear is everywhere. When is now and now is when. We boil in a pressure cooker of stress, a destiny of our own making and yet one that we reject, and now, yes now, finally we are overwhelmed by the futility of our own existence; it is then that we drink ourselves to oblivion to forget, to forgive and to forget the futility of our own futile flesh; and that time is now; because for many our existence is mere contradiction and all meaning is lost. Folly... folly... folly... it follows us irrespective of where we are, what we do, what we say, and therefore what we are, who we are, becomes irreducibly pointless.

The tape has stopped. It appeared a long silence followed this outburst. In truth, I was glad of the respite as my fingers ached from the rampant writing I had undertaken whilst taking notes. In truth, I had a fierce headache that refused to leave and I found it hard to concentrate. But the tape and computer were relentless, they did not care for the foibles of humanity and instead pursued their quest for questions with a relentless ease that I found most annoying.

'WHERE'

The man snorted derisively; judging from his

movements, he found this question humorous, although I knew not why. The sound of his voice laughing was disturbing; it was impossibly deep, undone, inhuman, yet filled with an irony that even the most experienced actor would have found hard to replicate. I was unsure but for a moment I believed that he would not answer the question, but at the very last moment his laughter fell silent and he began to speak,

'Where? Indeed! Where? Is it pertinent to change that around and instead ask *where from*? Or, if that perhaps does not make sense... hell... I'm drunk so what do I care if it makes sense or not... what was I saying... oh yes... perhaps it is better to say not where or where not... but where from. *Where from* is a much better question and dear room now you must listen, even to me a drunken waster who cares not for humanity or love, but yearns for decadence and destruction and to be free from the tyranny of a world of consumerism. When you understand *where from* then you will have the answer. NOW, I go for a kebab.... No more questions.

The video showed the man standing up; he crossed the room and kicked the tape machine from its place on the table. The sound stopped but I continued to watch, concerned, enthralled, and confused by what I was watching. I hadn't expected such immediacy, such vigour, and I was stunned. Momentarily, it looked like the man would make his way to the outside world with no further comment but at the last moment he turned with a rage-filled face and smashed his face into the video. The picture cut out. But not before I recognised the face. It was the face of a monster. It was a face of a beast. A face I never wanted to see again. It was my own...

If I Ruled the World

Nyfed Griffiths

'If I ruled the world,
Every day would be the first day of spring,
Every day I'd hear the sweet robin sing',
sang Harry Secombe on record.

If I ruled the world, what would I be? A president of the world or a prime minister of the world? Or Secretary General of the United Nations? But the United Nations doesn't seem to have much power. So the Secretary General of the United Nations wouldn't have much power either, perhaps. Or would I be a messiah or a maharishi, as there are in India, or something?

Whatever I'd be, what would I do? I don't think I'd do much different to what I do already. I'd talk to people, ask questions, make comments and probably write. I'd still be me whatever I'd do, or whatever I did, with all my weaknesses and strengths.

Harry Potter was advised to *'Play to your strengths'.* Shakespeare said: *'To thine own self be true'* or be true to yourself. I think that these exhortations are in tune with each other.

How would one play to one's strengths or be true to oneself? I believe, by following one's intuition and using one's experience. Our former creative writing tutor, Carole Morgan Hopkin, said that not everyone has a highly developed sense of intuition. However, I believe it is possible for everyone at the right time to use their intuition. This can be put in other ways: follow one's instinct, follow one's heart, follow one's nose, go by one's gut feeling, use one's common sense or even use one's uncommon sense. I believe that all these phrases say the same thing in different ways.

Whatever we do in life, we must learn. We can't but learn, once we *start* learning. And it can be said, though it sounds rather brutal: 'When you stop learning, you're dead.' In other words, when there's no more to learn, your time is up and the spirit must leave the physical body behind. Sometimes it may seem as if we are not learning, but I believe we are going through the process all the same. While we live and breathe, we *continue* to learn.

A teacher's maxim goes:
'What you hear, you forget,

What you see, you remember,
What you do, you know.'

Hearing and seeing are valuable, but doing, so says the maxim, results in knowing. When one sees something for oneself, then one understands. The greatest knowledge one can achieve is self knowledge – coming to know your inner self, the spirit within, the soul. Not for nothing did the ancient Greeks exhort *'Know thyself!'*

When I learn, I want to lead others to the same or a similar experience for them. I want to share – to capitalise on what I've learnt by helping others in their travail, if it be travail. If one is subject to it, I feel one needs to outgrow any mean or narrow-minded spirit. Encouraging a person at the right time is important. One needs to venture to imagine sometimes. To use one's ability in order to fulfil one's potential.

Jesus' words in the Bible say not to light a candle and put it under a bowl, but put it on a stand where it lights the whole house. They had small houses in those days with one room only. And also if you are given a talent, to use it, not to go and bury it in the ground, as in one of Jesus' parables.

Hywel Dda, a prince in Wales many centuries ago, ruled well and wisely and formulated fair and just laws. He had the laws administered soberly. He was a good ruler over his part of Wales. He used his ability and sense wisely. He used what God had given him wisely in my opinion.

To me, to rule the world doesn't necessarily mean to become an emperor and have an empire like Genghis Kahn, Napoleon Bonaparte, Adolf Hitler, the Roman Empire or the British Empire. Some of these were far flung empires, whether they were good or evil.

One way to rule the world is through conquering it by force of arms. I must say that I believe no empire is wholly evil, whatever its faults. There are other ways to rule the world, with ideas. A well-known saying is:

'The pen is mightier than the sword'.

Jesus, Mohammed, Moses, Gautama Buddha and Confucius influenced the world with their ideas. But none of these people were rulers, if I can use that term, of the whole world. They influenced part of it, however large. So can anyone rule the world, if these people in history didn't rule the whole world? People are different and some leaders appeal to some people rather than or more than to others.

God in his wisdom has sent different messengers to different parts of the world, throughout the ages. To me, Jesus was the person of greatest spiritual stature the earth has seen and will see, as he was described as the king of the angels – the king of heaven in a hymn.

The other leaders throughout time are also important, but Jesus is top dog as it were.

So, what if I ruled the world? I think I'd want everybody to follow the path of learning of life's spiritual lessons, which I believe is the purpose of life on earth anyway. And I also believe that everybody is destined to do this, helped by one's fellow man and woman. As the saying goes:

'When the student is ready, the master appears.'

To close with the words sung by Harry Secombe, that's what I'd do

'If I ruled the world.'

The Silence of the Grave

Lenni Charles

Blow Gabriel blow,
But not in my back yard,
No harps please
When I my mortal coil discard.
No pipers piping,
No gaggling of geese
Fear not the silence of this grave,
But think of a soul at peace.

There Will Come a Time

Rhian F. Miles

When there are no buttercups in the meadows, or primroses in the hedgerows, or periwinkle on the country lanes. There will come a time when there are no cows in the pasture, or pigs in the rough or sheep in the meadow. There will come a time when there will be no children playing hop-scotch, no fathers down the mines and no mothers pegging out the washing. There will come a time when the air once fresh and clear becomes obscured by fog, mist and pollution, where kiddies' lungs are full of blight and, instead of playing games, they huddle in their cots on dirty air scorched doorsteps. There will come a time when shopping becomes a passion of the past and mothers will buy only the bare necessities to make the bread and pies to fill their families' calling for food. There will come a time when there are no cars, vans, lorries, trains, planes, and Shanks' ponies called into use. There will come a time when schools will close, so too colleges and universities, and parents will become responsible for their children's education. Also a time when health centres, hospitals and residential homes will close, leaving Grandma's herb garden to medicate, and old people will be taken in by those with vacant rooms. The day approaches and one lives in fear of the darkness, death and destruction – and there will come a time when time itself runs out.

Some People Who've Influenced Me

Nyfed Griffiths

There are many people who've influenced me in my life, and I shall deal here, at least, with a few of them.

When I was a toddler, and later growing up to about the age of ten, we had a family of sisters living next door, who were retired teachers. One sister was married and lived with her husband next door to us, and in a semi-detached house next to theirs, at first, lived the other three sisters. I say at first, because one of the three died when I was very young. She was called Annie and I have very little recollection of her, in fact only an image in my mind.

I know that she had intended to tutor me personally, but she didn't live to realise her wish. I feel that she had taken a particular liking to me, wishing to give me lessons, for which I can only feel gratitude for her thoughtfulness and concern. I hope she can appreciate how I feel about her, up there in heaven.

Her death left Maggie and husband, Picton, and the *two* sisters, Gertie and Terry, next door. Although they were all Welsh and could speak the language, they habitually spoke English to each other and to me. That's how I picked up English at an early age. It has put me in good stead in the years that followed. In secondary school I was good at English essays and regularly got good marks. Indeed it has laid a basis for what was then my future.

I used to go through the gap in the hedge, between our house and their houses, often to visit them. I remember Maggie, the married sister, giving empty Corn Flakes and Quaker Oats packets to me, which had things to cut out on the backs. I think to begin with, she showed me how to cut these things out carefully. They were figures of cowboys and Indians and masks of animals perhaps, and famous people, like Co-Co the clown and Dick Turpin, the highway robber. Maggie nurtured me. These things were interesting, enjoyable and I found her and them inspiring.

Then there was Gertie, who lived in the semi-detached house next door to Maggie and her husband. She taught me to draw, by copying printed drawings, not with greaseproof paper, but with the eye – observing which way the line went, whether it was straight or curved and how long the straight or curved bits were. She also emphasised the shape of the drawing and its different parts and inculcated a sense of proportion in me. I was a willing student in their hands. It helped put my artistic skills on a good footing. Later on, in secondary school, I was to be regularly amongst the top three in my marks in art class. As a teenager I would make sketches in a sketch pad, while on summer holiday with my parents. As an adult in evening classes, I have made charcoal and chalk and pen and ink drawings, painted in acrylic and water colours. I liked the lady tutor we had then, too.

I want to mention my father briefly, while reviewing my art interest. When I was ill as a youngster, with colds and bronchitis up to the age of 16 (when I grew out of it), my father would also encourage me to draw or sketch, while sitting up in bed. I remember drawing a chair and the landscape scene I could see out of my bedroom window on one occasion.

So, I am indebted to these two ladies, sisters Maggie and Gertie, for starting me off with my English and artistic skills at an early age. I'm not sure whether the other sister, Terry, had been a teacher as well. She might have been required to stay at home while the other sisters teached.

After all the sisters died, Maggie's husband, Picton, tried to encourage my reading by giving me Reader's Digest magazines and letting me borrow any books the Reader's Digest might send to him. He would ask if I wanted to keep any of these books, and if I fancied a book he would let me have it, paying for it himself. I remember my father being concerned that I didn't read the books or that I infrequently read articles in the Reader's Digest magazines.

However, Picton's encouragement meant that from 1979 to 2006 I subscribed to Reader's Digest. That's over a quarter of a century. During that time I bought many Reader's Digest books, however much I read of them. But I remember finding several articles in the magazines that were worth reading, being well written and inspiring. They were often about some act of courage or perseverance in the face of seemingly insurmountable odds. That to me was, and still is, stirring stuff.

I owe these sisters and the husband a lot. If it hadn't been for them and the part they played in my life, I would be significantly poorer culturally and as far as self-expression goes. I wish to express my thanks to them, if it can reach them in the eternal realms on the other side of death. I would like them to know how I now feel towards them.

Perfect Love

Oskar Dremny

The 6 p.m. train from London Paddington to Penzance sat at the station in a cloud of steam, oil and diesel fumes. The train was painted Brunel dark blue, the passenger carriages were blue but with a white stripe that ran along the length of the carriage, and the train was so long that the carriages followed the curve of the platform and disappeared out of sight around the corner. The train platform was a hive of activity: suitcases scraped across the floor, rucksacks jostled on the entrance steps to train carriages, and all the while thousands of commuter shoes looked forward to the long rest home. The passengers rushed along the platform in search of that ever elusive perfect seat. All seats on this train are not equal.

In Seat 3E of carriage G, an unsightly man smiled to himself as he read *The Times* newspaper. He was content as he had found a good seat: during rush-hour it had become harder and harder to find a seat with a table if you did not reserve your seat prior to departure, and he was happy as with a table he could lay the paper on it and read without being cramped or confined. Unconsciously, he checked his watch anxiously.

The man sincerely believed that he was ugly: he had chipped teeth, over-sized ears, an eye that was slightly lower than the other, a birthmark just behind his right ear, and a slight but nonetheless prominent bald patch, and then there were the burns. He didn't want to think about the burns. They were everywhere.

He had finished his paper, except it wasn't his, it was just a well read copy of *The Times* that had been on the seat when he arrived so he had picked it up and started to read. He often found newspapers discarded on the seat like that. It didn't matter what kind of paper they were just as long as he could read, as to read, to lose himself in a splendid piece of news, or sport, helped to take his mind off the train. The plain featured man loved and yet hated the train, because whilst it had been a constant presence throughout his life, somehow he was stuck in an internal struggle to understand how the train affected him.

Anxiously, he checked his watch, unconsciously eager for the train to get under way so that he could finally relax. He felt tense whilst he had nothing to do, and it was only when the gentle movement of the train began that he would feel comfortable enough to let go of the tension that kept him alert and safe. He gazed sadly at the empty seat opposite him. It was unusual that a person would sit face to face with him on a journey unless the train was completely full and there was literally nowhere else to sit, and during the last few years he had begun to feel morose and sad about his lack of friends. In an effort to compensate he watched other people as they enjoyed their companionships: friends on the way to a night out, lovers who were curled up tight against each other's bodies with a casual arm here and there, or perhaps strangers who had just met and were sharing a piece of gossip on the way home from work. The repellent man had reached a stage in his life where he was tired of being alone and sad that he never had the opportunity to share his narratives, his own adventures.

Most people found him repulsive and chose to avoid him; or alternatively they would blatantly stare at him until at last, even though he tried very hard not to let them upset him, he could not return their gaze and lowered his eyes. It was not his fault. Unfortunately, when he was a child he had been in a terrible train crash. The impact and twisted wreckage had killed his father instantly and when his father had died, he had taken with him to heaven the mind of his mother, and she had spent the rest of her days raving mad at the loss of her husband; as for him, he was very nearly burnt to death.

The doctors had said it was a miracle and they had praised the wonder of modern medical science. It didn't feel like a miracle. To him it felt like a curse but his therapist disagreed and said in her strange voice that 'it was good for him to get on the train; positive experiences would help relieve the negativity that he associated with the past', but the disfigured man doubted such mumbo jumbo would work.

He guessed that the train would be leaving soon as he could sense a change in the sound of the engines; he would be glad when the train was under way. To cope with the emotional uncertainty that being sat here created, the unlovely man loved to people-watch: everyone was so different, so diverse, different noses, teeth, hair, smiles, eyes, and some even more interesting areas that he could not mention. He often wondered why he was the only displeasing man on the train; when he was tired and felt low he was incredibly jealous of the tall, handsome type of man who sat with a beautiful woman and chatted with ease. During his convalescence, in the first decade after the crash, he had prayed every day. He had asked God if he could arrange for a very unattractive girl to get on the train, and more specifically could he arrange that she sit next to him, so that he could talk to her and share some form of human contact that didn't involve doctors, nurses, or therapists, but eventually, after many months of waiting, he realised that God had not answered. That bitter realisation meant that his Christian faith faded into the background. Instead, he placed his faith in coincidence. Perhaps one day he would bump into a girl who had a birthmark or a scar on her face, a misshapen girl who wouldn't be afraid of him, a girl he could talk to and pass the time with pleasantly.

The ill-favoured man loved stories. Invariably, if he wasn't people-watching then he would spend his time imagining stories, as there was something about the gentle motion of the train that stimulated his imagination. At that very moment, the guard standing on the platform blew his whistle, a final rucksack squeezed past the last open door, and the train began to pull away. The blue carriages began to pick up speed as commuter shoes settled down to rest, and the ghastly man sat back with a content grin as his imagination kicked into life.

Sometimes if he felt anxious, and he normally did when he was on the train, then he would imagine a terrible train crash: the carriages would be heaved, twisted, torn, metal shredded and broken, glass shattered into shards, and foam seat cushions melted as heat slammed through the train, some carriages caught fire, disintegrated, or exploded; but fortunately for him he was always thrown clear through a glass-free window. Courageously he returned, ignoring his cuts and bruises, to help the passengers to safety. It was inevitable that some people would die, or be badly burned like he had been, but he would help the living to escape and in return they would become his life-long friends. He knew that it was depressing to be so lonely that he had to imagine these things but a small part of him just couldn't bear the loneliness and hence he forgave himself these dark wonderings of the imagination. Of course, they weren't always dark, if it were a good day then he would imagine that a...

A girl brushed past his shoulder and threw a crumpled rucksack down on the window seat opposite him; it was green and purple with an 'I love Australia' sticker on its left side. She looked funky. The young woman wore bright pink trousers, with a curious woollen jumper, which had a picture of a dog on it, and she had blond hair that curled down to her shoulders. She had a kind but inquisitive face and looked at him curiously, as if undecided on whether or not to sit there, and then squinted at the pages of a small book that nestled in her hand. She smiled and then self-consciously brushed her hair from her face, and spoke rapidly:

'*Hola Señor! Es este el tren para Penzance?*' she asked, tired but needing to sit down.

The no-oil-painting man was nonplussed by this sudden outburst: he looked at her for a while as if unsure how to proceed and then just grinned and shrugged his shoulders. The girl had realised that she had used the wrong language and smiled in embarrassment, 'Sorri,' she hesitated with a thick Spanish accent, and then checked her book again. 'Is this seat used?' she asked.

'Used?' the grisly man laughed, 'I should say! This train is older than me... but I take it that what you really mean to say is, is this seat empty?' and he indicated the seat in question, mighty curious that she might even sit opposite him.

The girl absorbed what he had said and then squinted closely at the book whilst she turned the pages this way and that until eventually she looked up.

'*Si! Gracias Señor*, I is meaning this,' she said with a weary grin. More than anything in the world, she just needed to sit down and rest her aching legs, for no one had told her that travelling was so hard and laborious. The very pretty girl stretched and yawned with her hands high above her head, which in turn lifted up the bottom of her jumper and showed just an inch of flat tummy. She was totally oblivious that her beauty made the man feel grotesque and monstrous: here he was slumped in his chair, his hair was a mess, he hadn't shaved – the stubble was ill-kempt and patchy – or washed, so his skin felt greasy and tired, his ears were waxy and dirt ridden; at least he had cleaned his teeth, he was pleased about that, although he was not actually sure when it was he had last cleaned them. He desperately wanted to rearrange himself and needed to go and smarten up.

Meanwhile, the young lady had finished yawning and disappointingly the flat tummy had disappeared. 'Can I be sitting here?' she asked, after she had checked the book once more and decided that *yes* she had got the correct words this time.

'Yeah you can sit here if you want,' he shrugged, conscious that he didn't want to appear too keen and therefore really trying hard to appear relaxed and neutral, but inwardly his mind raced, 'Yes! Of course yes! A million times yes! Sit here my wonderful beauty. Sit here with me and I will show you England in all her glory.'

But outwardly, he said nothing and there was no hint of his excitement except for a rather unusual highly erect left eyebrow, which had developed a mind of its own and now wriggled for attention.

The young woman plonked herself into the seat opposite him and smiled, happy that she had found a seat on the train. Her feet ached as she had walked from Liverpool Street to Paddington because she was trying to save money and also because she had wanted to see the sights of London.

The train had been late but she was not sure why as she had lost her contact lenses – they must have fallen out of her bag as she couldn't find them anywhere – and hence she had been unable to read the signs at the terminal, so instead she had just found the platform and then sat down for a rest whilst she waited for the train to arrive. Losing her contact lenses was a pain because they were expensive but it wasn't the end of the world; she had a pair of glasses in her rucksack, although she had decided not to wear them as she didn't want to look like a geek; she had been teased about her glasses at school and now only wore them in a real emergency. In *her* mind, sitting on a train was not a real emergency.

In reality, she could see most things, like outlines anyway, just no real detail. It didn't matter anyhow as she was going to go to sleep. She wondered why the train had been delayed, and thought perhaps the man opposite her might know.

'*Por-ke-sa-le-el-tren-kon-re-traso*?' she asked, and then blushed when she realised that she had forgotten to speak English again, and started to search for her book.

The ugly man laughed. He had no idea what she was talking about but he wasn't that bothered. She looked so attractive speaking that language. He looked deeply into her green eyes; they seemed endlessly deep and welcoming but she had a tendency to squint which was rather disconcerting and it made her face bunch up a little. He tried not to stare because she was so stunning. Happily, he would have listened to her chatter on all day. Who cared what she said? He didn't mind that her English was poor; it would be fun trying to teach her. Her voice cut through his thoughts. Damn, she was talking to him and he was too busy procrastinating.

'Sorry? What was that?' he asked, worried that he had missed something important.

The girl looked up from her book and frowned in concentration.

'Why is the tran delayed?' she asked, simply.

'Tran?' he asked, not entirely clear what she meant. She pointed at the carriage all around them.

'Oh, you mean train!' he laughed unselfconsciously, and decided to try and brush his hair into some sort of order with his hands.

She returned his smile with a grin that hinted at hidden treasures 'Train. *Si Señor*... Why is the train delayed?'

He shrugged, non-committal, 'Someone got shot on the tube.'

'Shot, *Señor*? What is this shot?' she asked, not understanding.

'How do I explain that the police have just killed a man?' he thought for a moment and then decided that it was perhaps best that he didn't explain. London wasn't really a great place to be at the moment and he didn't really want to talk about it, so he decided to change the subject.

'Are you learning English?' he said, trying to change the subject. He was beginning to wonder why she had sat with him.

The girl nodded at his question and held up the small phrase book, '*Si Señor*, I is learning English but I is very bad,' she replied, ruefully.

He smiled and decided to stop worrying about why she had sat here opposite him and instead to try and relax and just enjoy the moment. 'I think your English is not as bad as my Spanish?' he offered with a wry grin, and then tried to rearrange his body in a more attractive position. He hoped that she would notice.

'You is speaking Spanish?' she asked with a squint, but didn't notice that he had moved, as she could barely see that far.

'No, I don't speak Spanish... but I would like to learn,' he replied, looking for a way to get to know this girl.

'Spanish is easy to learn,' she said quickly. 'You is wanting me to teach you?'

'Are you kidding,' the unattractive man thought to himself, 'I would love for you too teach me. You can teach me Spanish as well if you want, he grinned to himself. She was a beauty. He couldn't believe his luck.

'Sure that would be great,' he said, careful not to appear too eager, but his left eyebrow once more had become erect and began to wriggle around of its own accord.

The young woman grinned, squinted at him and then began to look in her phrase book as she wanted to chat to this man because he seemed nice and gentle. Most men would have been flirting like mad with her by now; she felt relieved that he seemed a little shyer than most men. She needed to find the correct words and so kept flicking through the pages, until she found what she was looking for. In truth, she wished now that she had listened to her mother and purchased the larger book, but at the time she had been too excited about the trip to worry about things like that.

'What words is you wanting to speak?' she asked, after her book consultation was complete. The young man looked at her and grinned. He knew exactly what he wanted to learn.

'How do I say hello?' he asked. She laughed, 'That is too easy. To say hello you is saying *hola*...'

'*Hola* is hello?' he asked.

'Yes, *hola* is saying hello,' she replied, pleased that they were communicating in Spanish.

The unlovely man yawned and then tried to stretch in a sexy way like the girl but somehow it didn't quite work, and it actually made him look more hideous, so he stopped and then scratched his head in the place where he had been burnt as a child. It itched terribly but not as much as his lower body where the very worst of the burns had been; he tried to ignore the dull ache pervading his legs courtesy of Great Western Railway seats and instead concentrated on the conversation.

'You're right, that is too easy... how do I say... good morning?' he asked, hoping that she had not noticed the un-sexy stretching. He loved her smile. It was invigorating. He just wanted to watch that smile forever.

'You tease me,' she grinned, and it was obvious that she either hadn't been looking or that she just didn't find him ugly. 'Everybody is knowing that good morning is *buenos días*!'

'*Bwen-as-dee-oss!*' he tried the words out but they didn't sound right.

'Nooo... not *oss*... you says it wrong... it's *buenos días*!'

'*Bwen-os-dee-ASS*,' he repeated softly, the word ass holding a completely different connotation to the meaning of good morning that she had intended.

He sat up and shifted his legs to stop them going numb on the seat. His lower scars ached terribly, and the motion of the train seemed to transmit itself to every part of his tired body. The train hit a bump and he almost tipped forward across the table.

'Woah! Sorry...' he muttered, but not very sincerely.

His retina had captured a close up image of her that had burned into his eyes: her face with its bemused smile, the curve of her neck, the soft looking skin, the delicate green eyes that hinted of unknown pleasure, the soft lips with just a hint of mid-sentence tongue behind them, the swell of her chest hidden demurely beneath a white pullover; it was an image that he would keep forever.

When he had nearly fallen across the table the girl's eyes had widened, not in fear, well not in his opinion, but rather with interest. The man decided to raise the stakes a little.

'OK, I have another question?' he said simply.

'*Si! Si!*' she giggled, conscious that she couldn't see much, so she had decided that a giggle here and there would save face. Most men, in her experience, were happy as long as you pretended to listen to their every word and then giggled at the appropriate moment.

'How do you say...' he paused, suddenly unsure if he could say something like this to a woman such as her. He had never even begun to flirt with a woman before. What if she got angry and decided to leave. That would have been terrible.

'Yes?' she asked, prompting him with her fingers, making little movements that encouraged him.

He noticed that she had gentle soft looking hands. Perhaps, those hands could... but he banished the thought before it really got started and concentrated on his question. He grinned nervously, 'How do you say, you're a beautiful woman?'

The Spanish girl flicked through her book a few times, and kept repeating the words in her head so that she wouldn't forget them until she translated them. She blushed when she had worked out what the strange words meant; the compliment was clear but unexpected and a little awkward as she didn't really go for men. And now was no exception, but inwardly a part of her smiled and momentarily she thought to herself 'how charming', and then involuntarily she yawned and stretched and showed just a little bit more flat tummy and suddenly felt very sleepy and so sat back in her chair and got comfy; she really was quite tired after her travelling.

'*Tu estas una mujer muy* Linda,' she replied with a sleepy voice in answer to his question.

The ugly man nodded but didn't attempt to repeat the words. He stared at her tummy. It was a thing of beauty, of wonder, of lust and of desire, and the soft skin, smooth and unblemished, made him feel funny somewhere deep inside himself. Unconsciously, he scratched the scars on his face.

He wanted to talk, he really did, but he didn't really trust his mouth to say anything of consequence at that particular moment. He just wanted to stare at her beauty and allow it to wash over him. He knew that it was wrong to stare, some would say it was uncivilised and impolite, but he just wanted to make the most of it while it lasted. Hence, he decided it was better to pretend to be cool and wait for her to talk.

The girl's eyes were weary and tender. It hurt having to squint all the time without her glasses so she closed them for just a few moments. It was nice to rest after her long journey and she decided that she would sleep for a while, as the train was going to take a long time to get to the destination.

The plain man could not believe that this girl had spoken to him. Now that she had closed her eyes, he leant forward and watched her. The motion of the train continued to rock the carriage and the clatter of the wheels echoed from underneath the train. By the time the train had reached Reading, the girl was fast asleep.

The slightly ordinary man, at least he felt ordinary: ordinary after his conversation with this girl, ordinary because she had smiled at him with genuine warmth, ordinary because she had laughed at the things he had said, and just plain ordinary because he had forgotten his woes, forgotten his burns, forgotten how ugly he thought he was and instead he just was ordinary and that in itself was fine. He sat in his chair his left eyebrow still erect and unbelievably excited but with a growing sense of fatigue; finally, the motion of the train comforted him and his eyes waned until he too fell fast asleep.

The 6:15 p.m. train from London Paddington to Penzance thundered along the track at almost one hundred miles an hour in a cloud of steam, oil and diesel fumes. The diesel engine roared with the strain and burnt gallons of fuel every second as it pulled along the passenger carriages that were blue with a white stripe that ran along the length of them. Now and then the wheels clattered and clanked against an uneven piece of iron on the track. No one heard the clank that sounded rather unusual as the train hit a broken piece of track: not the driver who was reading his paper whilst he drove, nor the conductor who was trying to free an elderly lady from the toilet, nor the lonely young man who had sat on the train to Penzance reading someone else's paper, but inexorably, without drama or noise, the train slowly began to derail.

An Autobiographical Account

Nyfed Griffiths

I started my spiritual journey in about 1954, at the age of seven years old in London. My father, my mother and myself were visiting my mother's eldest sister, Rachel or Auntie Rae as I knew her. She was a nurse in a factory in London and was separated from her husband. She had a man friend called Harry.

I remember particularly one day of our holiday in London. In the morning we had gone out to the city and we'd had something to eat and drink in a little café. I think I had my first milk shake there. It was lovely. There was a nice lady serving us at the bar. We left and I was last and as we disappeared, she came to the window and motioned for me to come back. I hesitated and she motioned again and I left my relatives and went back into the café. The lady gave me a paper bag with the name of the café on it.

My relatives had missed me and wondered where

I'd gone. I soon came running after them with the paper bag and explained that the lady wanted me to come back for the paper bag that she had given me.

I don't quite remember whether my aunt had asked me if I'd said thank you for the bag, and whether she went back to the café to thank the lady for it.

It was after this that I first remember hearing a voice, what I shall call telepathy. I think it was my aunt's voice I heard. She wondered if I *knew*. She decided that I didn't and realised I was just then starting upon my seventy-year spiritual journey. I think I was seven or eight. I can't remember exactly.

I think my aunt asked if I wanted to know. I realised there was something *to* know and said in my thought that I did. She asked if I wanted to be able to do a lot of things now and have some understanding, or whether I would be willing to suffer a lot first – in ignorance – and then be able to do things and understand, towards the end of my life. I wondered what to do. She sensed my wonderment and said telepathically that the latter was better.

I decided on the second course, upon which she stated by telepathy that I was good – that is, a good person. As you know there are good and bad people. I am one of the former. All this happened through telepathic conversation.

I think she said that I could start what is my spiritual journey. I heard her say in Welsh or English, in my mind – I don't remember which language – 'He's starting!'

I think during this brief spell of telepathy my father might have been involved too, as Aunty Rae might have addressed him telepathically as well. I think Aunty Rae observed at some stage in this telepathic discourse: 'He's big' and maybe 'He's very special', about me.

And that was my first experience of telepathy and the beginning of my spiritual journey. I think my aunt knew, she realised, that I was going to suffer terribly, but that all would come right at the end. But I'm not dead yet. I still have about fifteen years or so to go, I reckon.

On reflection it was as if the lady in the café had, in giving me the paper bag, given me the keys to the kingdom. And that she acted as a high priestess and then handed me over to my aunt, another high priestess, and my father, who also knew what it was all about. I mean high priestesses as far as the spiritual life goes and the *secrets* of life, as Jesus had taught about the abiding principles of life, which he knew full well. It was like an initiation ceremony, but totally innocuous. I still feel even now that there's an air of mystery, intrigue and secrecy about it all.

We all have to tread this path some time or other, whatever our religion or belief or lack of it. Each must follow his or her own path, and will come upon or meet the right people at the right time.

* * *

Whatever Happened To?

Anonymous

Whatever happened to the suave, sophisticated older men?
There aren't any anymore.

Whatever happened to the world getting bigger and better?
It seems to be shrinking somehow.

Whatever happened to the excitement of staying at all-night parties and meeting interesting people?
It all seems so shallow. Have people changed or am I just growing older with jaded tastes?

Whatever happened to the enthusiasm for posh hotels?
They're all so impersonal and they can't cook as well as I can.

Whatever happened to young people striving for their dreams or old people remembering the 'good old days'?

Love is sissy and spelt 'luv'. People are afraid to be nice to each other in case it's misinterpreted as 'coming on'. Eight-year-old girls are sex objects and nine-year-old boys are gangsters.

Whatever happened to Mum and Dad, Gran, and the old girl down the road?

Whatever happened to hope, opportunity and trust and the feeling of security in banks and hospitals and on the streets?

Whatever happened to us?

Snail Pace

Rhian F. Miles

Down in the bottom of the garden lived a little snail called Brian. He loved to slither and slide under the cracked door of the garden shed (whether Grandpa was in residence or not), and slip in and out of the tools and things on the floor. Grandpa used to escape to the green shed when he wanted to be alone and far from the demands of everyday life! On the floor were bottles of home-brewed beer, and Brian enjoyed the privilege of 'slurping' the beer when the bottle exploded. It was Grandpa's job to tidy up the glass fragments before anyone got hurt, and then, when all the jobs were done, he was able to open his own little bottle of beer.

Grandpa enjoyed pottering about in the rhubarb patch and cutting stalks for Grandma to make into a pie. The gooseberries too, once harvested, went into jars and gooseberry wine. So did the blackcurrants, which made lovely jams, preserves, pies, and wine too. In the orchard, they also had an abundance of apple and pear trees, and the children (when they were called) would collect up the fallen fruits and eat, and eat, until their bellies were fair swollen.

Grandpa was fascinated with the saliva trails he saw in the shed early every morning, and could see that the trails went round and round and round in circles, where the beer had been spilt. The colours of the trails were rainbow hues (like petrol in water), where the purple and blues made waves amidst the pinks and the whites, and he would pick up a bamboo cane and swizzle the colours until mystical forms took place in the puddle. Because of the beauty from this, Grandpa decided to fulfil the snail's ardour by leaving a shallow cup (made from cut-off lemonade bottles) full of beer on the floor every night. His favourite snail, which he also called Brian (and he was right), he painted on his shell with the letter 'B', and he was special because Grandpa had painted him silver. Grandpa would look forward to seeing Brian, whilst he ate his rounds of toast and marmalade and a flask of tea, in the shed.

When they all came to visit, Grandpa would line them all up on the floorboard and place bets on who was going to win the race from the open shed door to the garden rake. Sometimes he would nudge the snails with his broom handle because they were so lazy and would not race. Sometimes, he would dip a rag in the beer and dab it on the snails' horns to encourage them to race. One thing was sure, and that was that Grandpa would always win the bets. A special bond had developed between him and the snails, and every day he set his alarm at daybreak, just as the light was breaking through the night, and he would get washed and dressed ready for another adventure and another day. One particular day disaster struck; as Grandpa approached his pied-a-terre, he saw the green door open and hanging on its hinges. He very carefully looked and saw his bottles had been stolen, and his friends (Brian and co), were nowhere to be seen. He searched and searched but to no avail, and then he spied a corner of a note peeping out from under a cracked flowerpot. On it was written quite clearly for Grandpa to see a cryptic verse:

'Sorry old man; and also madam – I've taken away the escargot. I raced and I chased, and I ate them all up, and now there's no escargot embargo!'

The Stuff of Dreams

Nyfed Griffiths

I am aware that some people may not be enthusiastic or as enthusiastic as I am about spaceflight. It doesn't excite some people like it excites me. I am fervent about men and women going into space.

Although I doubt very much whether NASA (the National Aeronautics and Space Administration) or the European Space Agency (ESA) would have me as an astronaut, I can conceivably think of going into space for a few minutes of weightlessness with Sir Richard Branson in one of his Virgin Galactic spaceships, due to fly in 2009, provided I had the necessary money sometime. It would cost about £114,000 I believe.

Such a flight would only be sub-orbital – looping up into space for a few minutes, to return again to Earth without having gone into orbit. Beggars can't be choosers, so this would satisfy me.

I delight in hearing space news, particularly

manned spaceflight news. I'm glad that Britain has launched a satellite – way back in 1971 – and that we have had a British astronaut launched into space as a British citizen (not under the auspices of joint nationality with the United States). That was Helen Sharman, called 'the woman from Mars' (as she worked for the Mars chocolate bar company), in May 1991. She went up in a Russian Soyuz spacecraft for about an six-day stay on the Russian Mir space station. (Hers was an eight-day flight, taking two days to reach space station Mir after launch from Baikonur Cosmodrome in Kazakhstan.)

I don't decry the achievement of the British–American joint nationality astronauts either. There was Michael Foale, the second British astronaut, following Helen Sharman. He helped save a potentially life-threatening situation, when a spacecraft hit the orbiting Mir space station on which he was aboard in June 1996. Another two similarly joint nationality British astronauts have been in space. They were the third and fourth British astronauts, Piers Sellers and Nicholas Patrick. But our Helen was the first Briton in space.

I said Britain had launched a satellite into space. The first nation to launch a satellite into space was the Soviet Union (now Russia) on October 4, 1957, with the famous Sputnik with its 'bleep bleep' signal. The second country to join the space club was the USA in January 1958. They were followed by France in 1965, Japan in

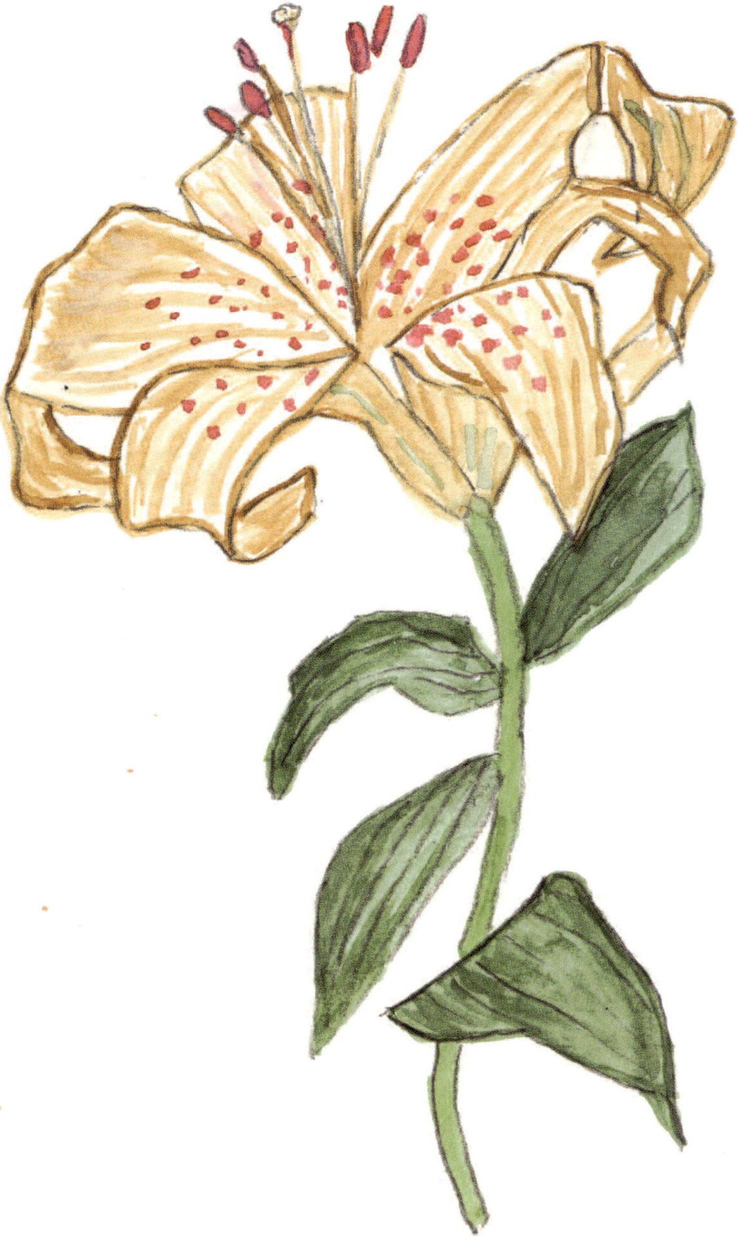

Martin Burke

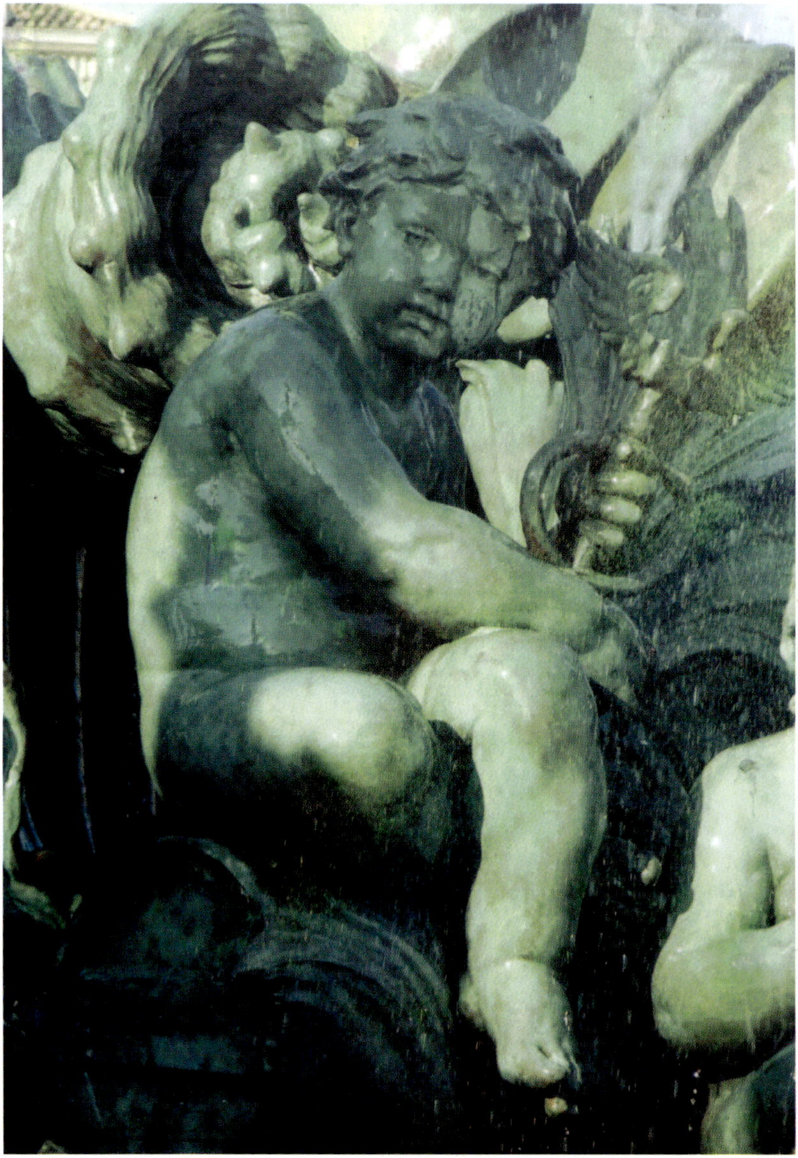

Ceri Pugh

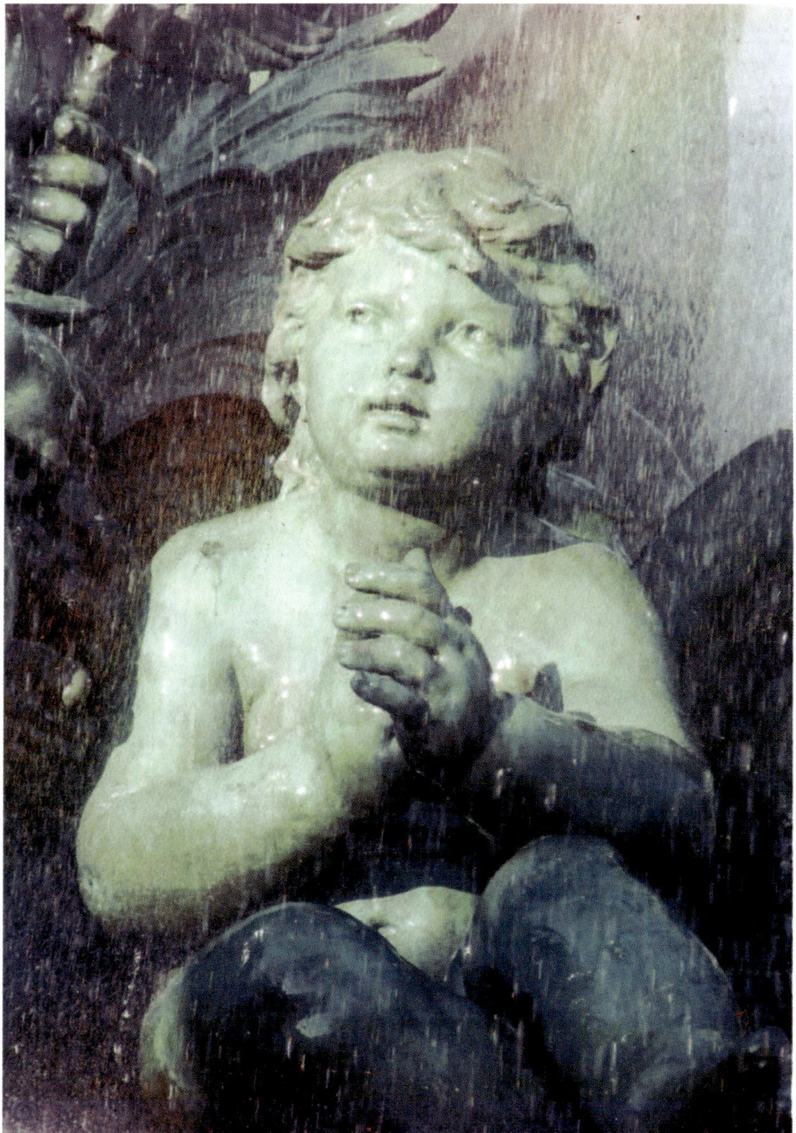

Ceri Pugh

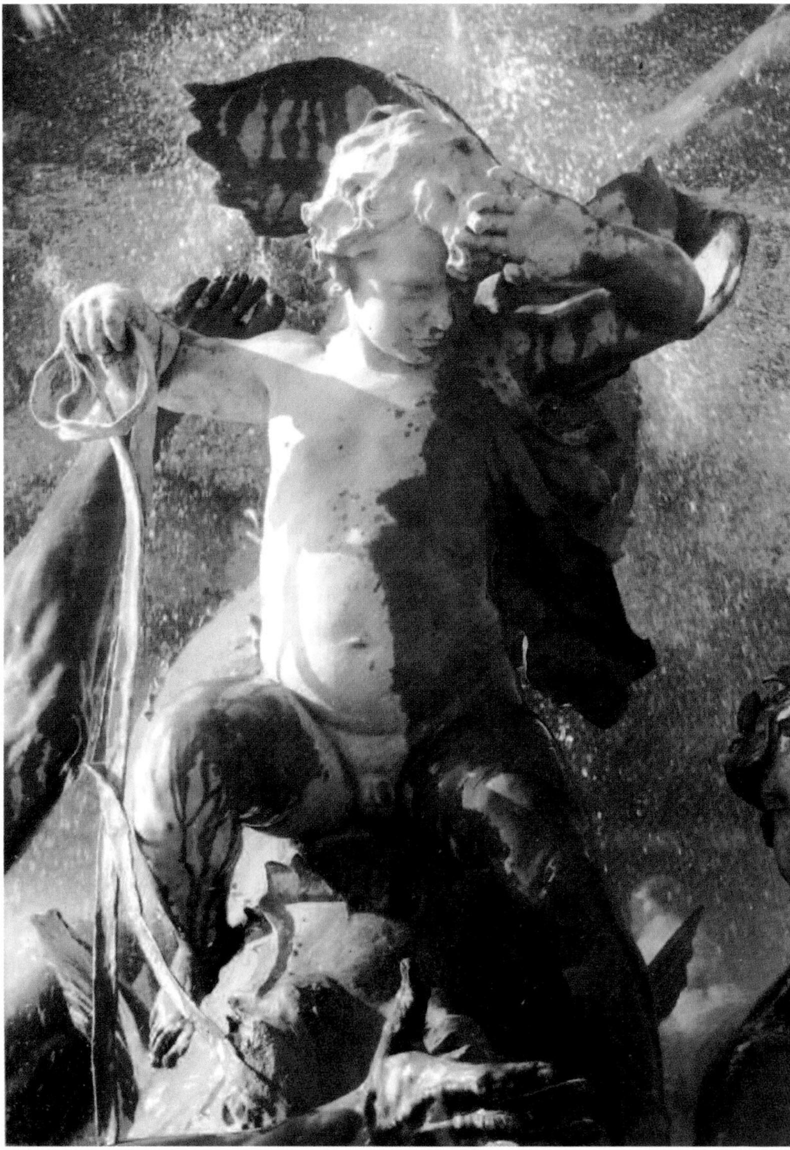

Ceri Pugh

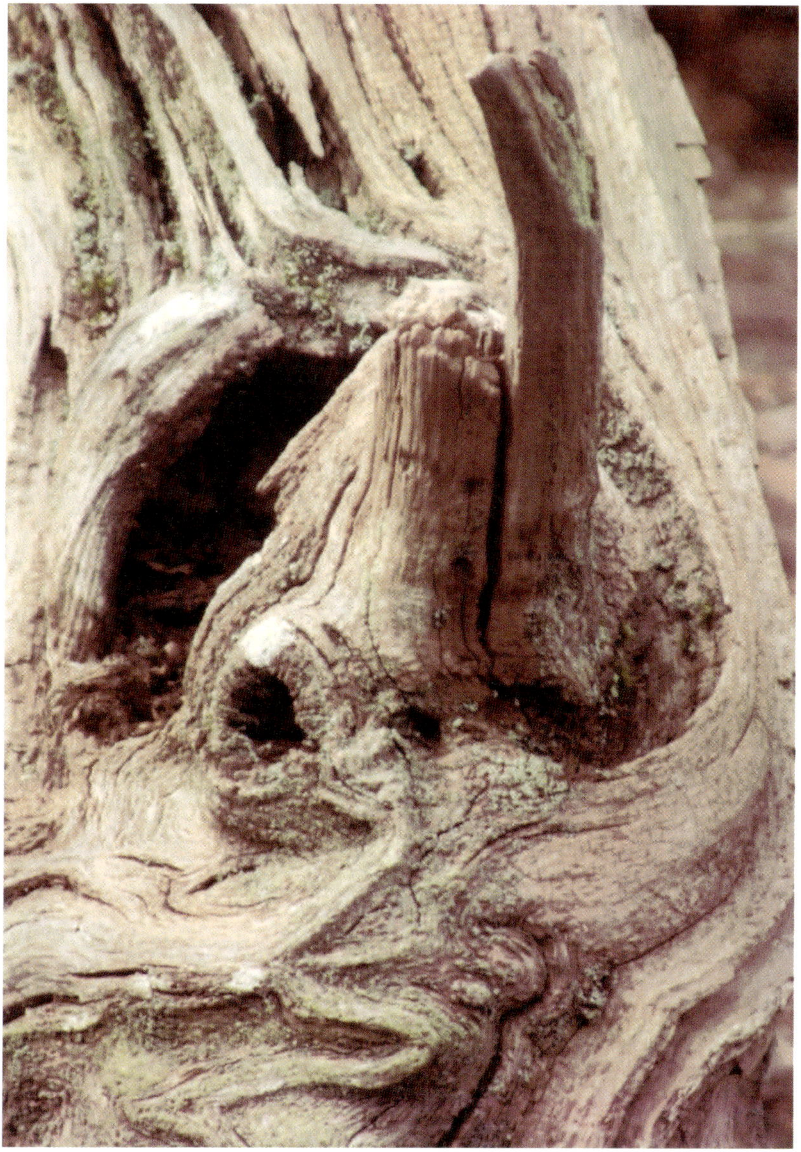

Ceri Pugh

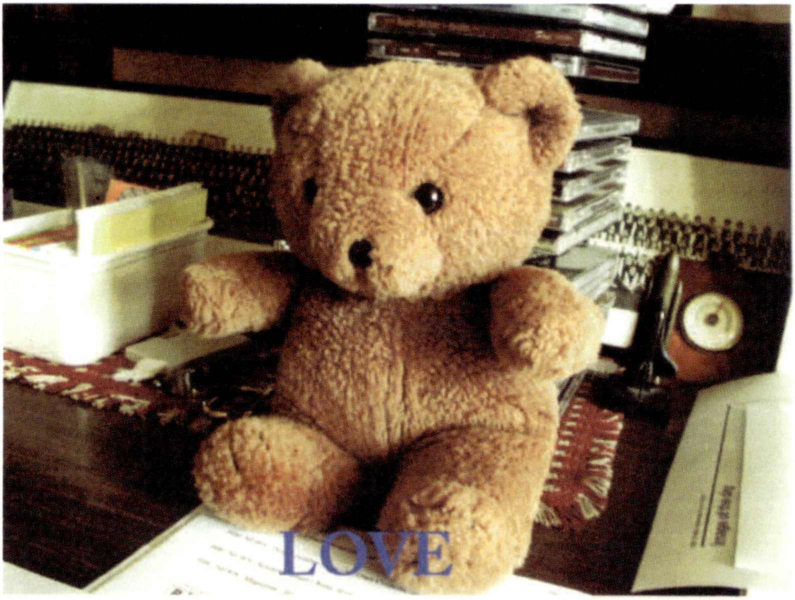

Nyfed Griffiths

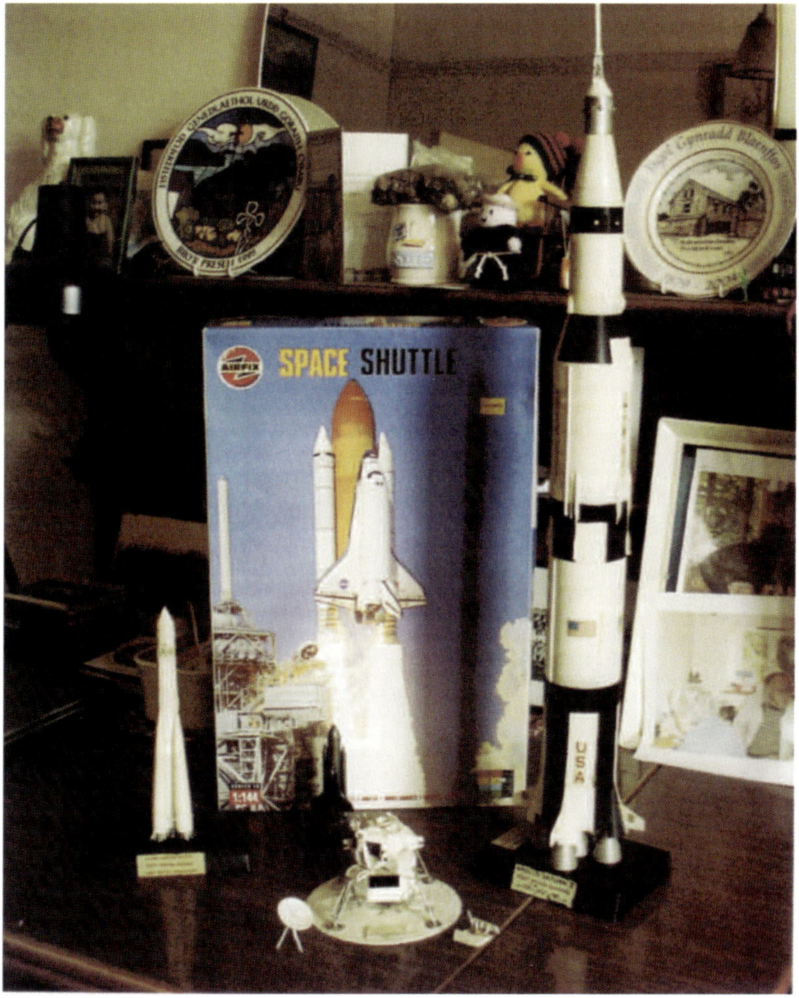

Nyfed Griffiths

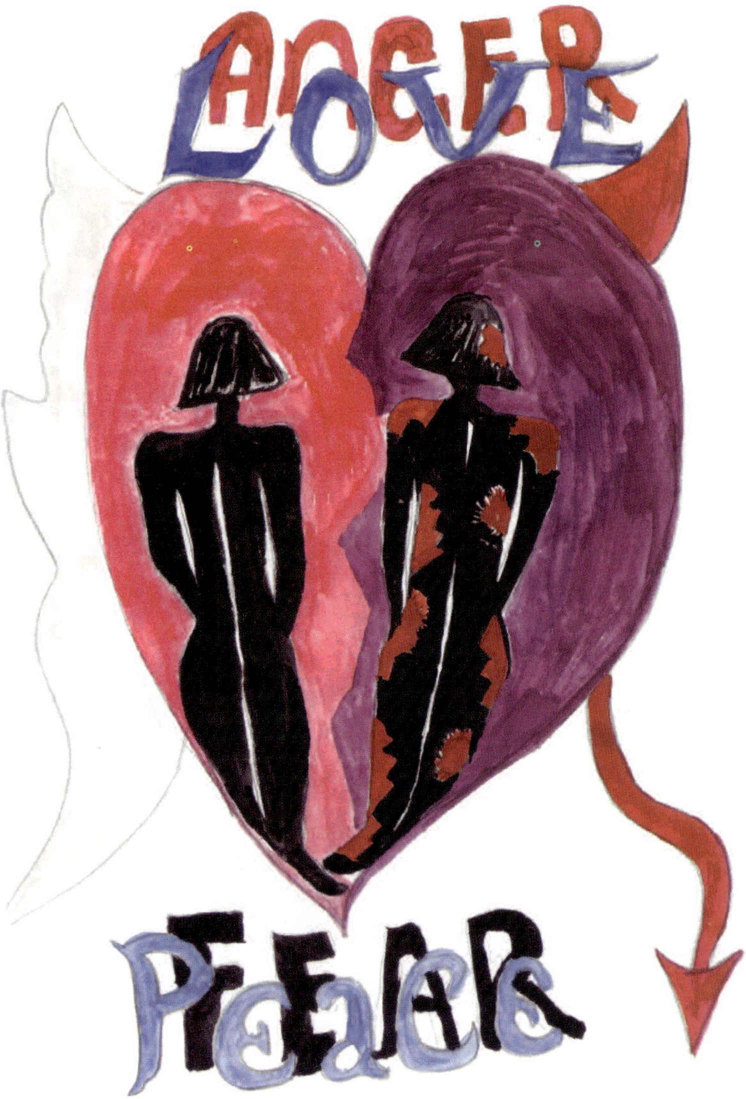

Elizabeth Davies

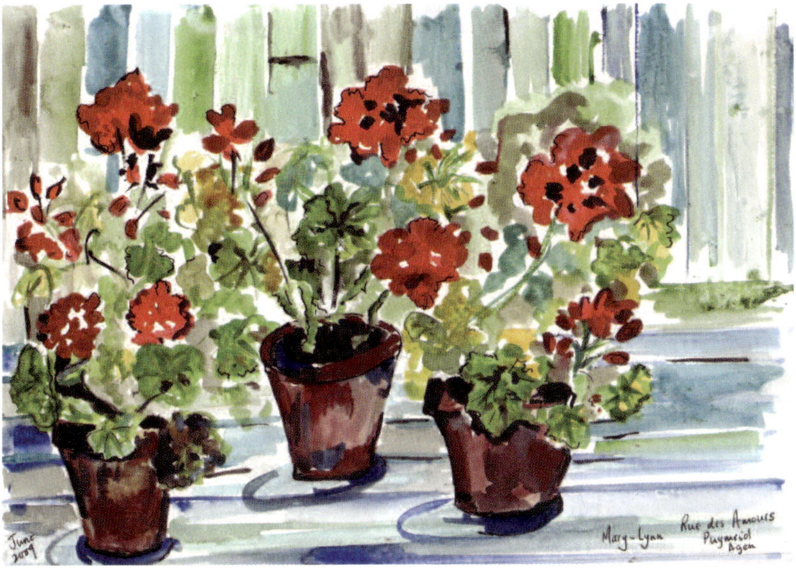

Lynn Davies

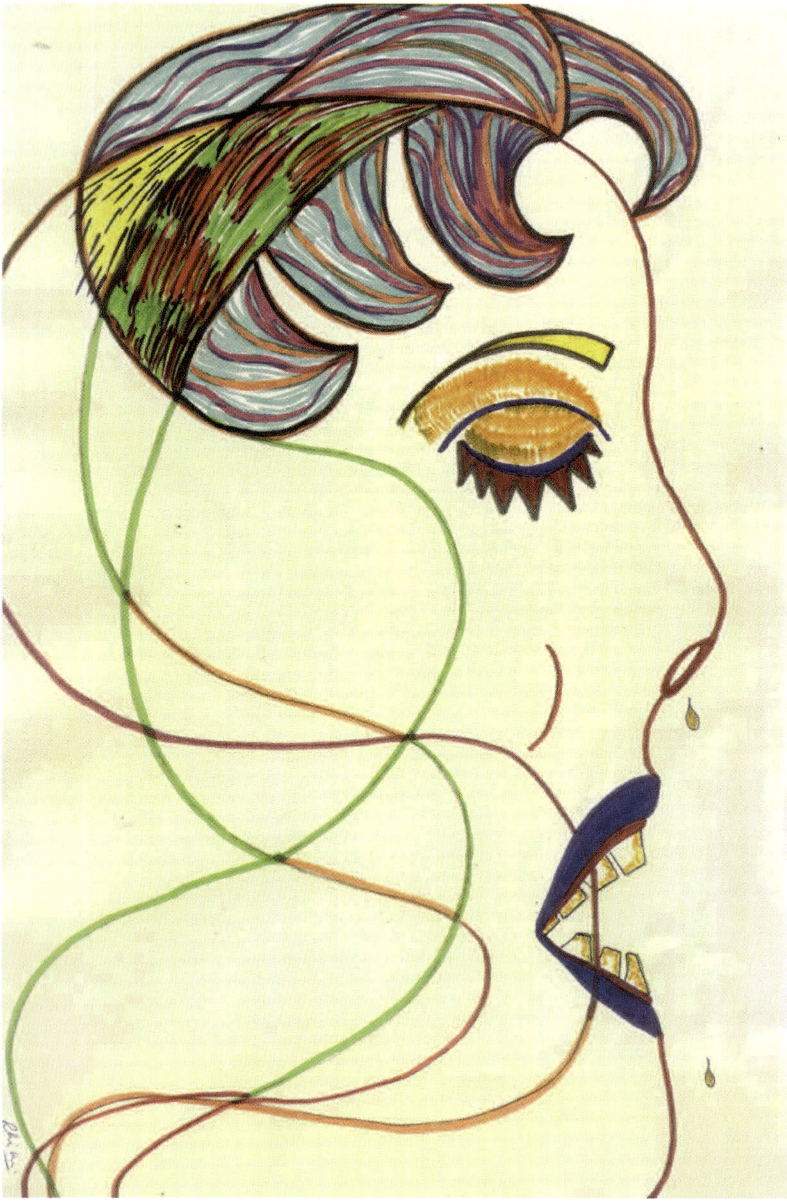

Rhian F. Miles

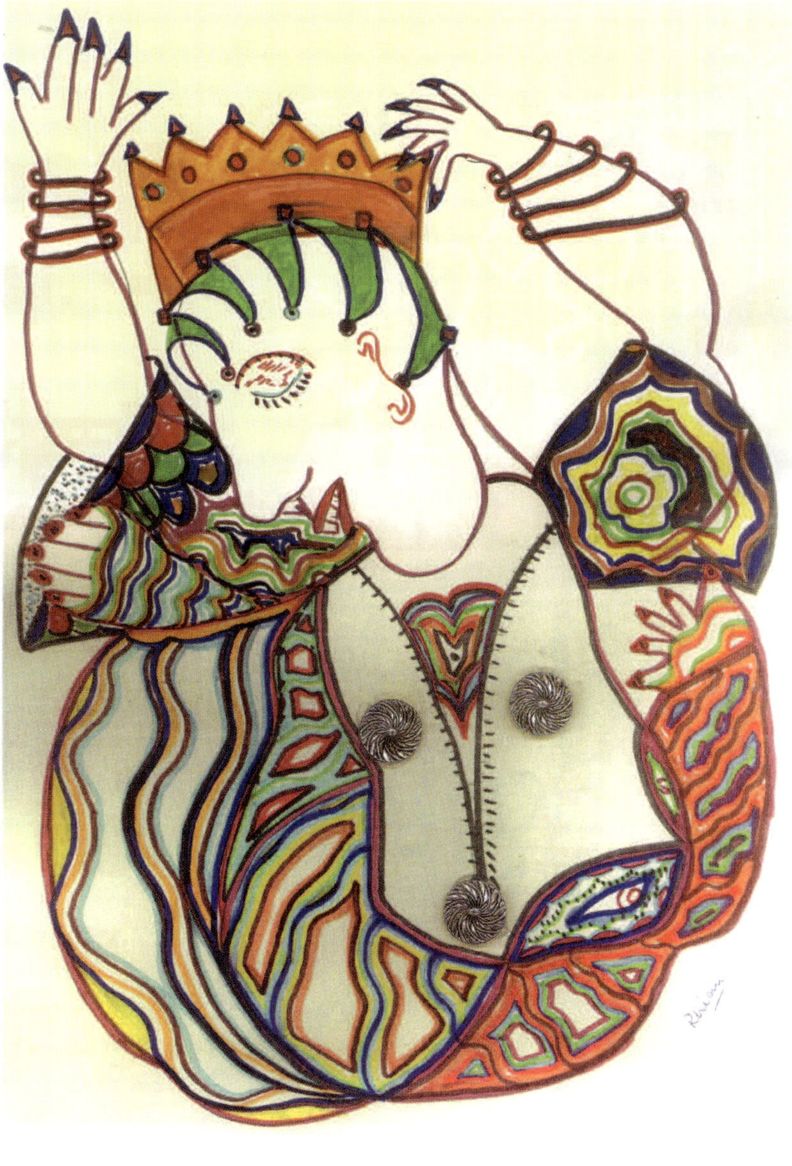

Rhian F. Miles

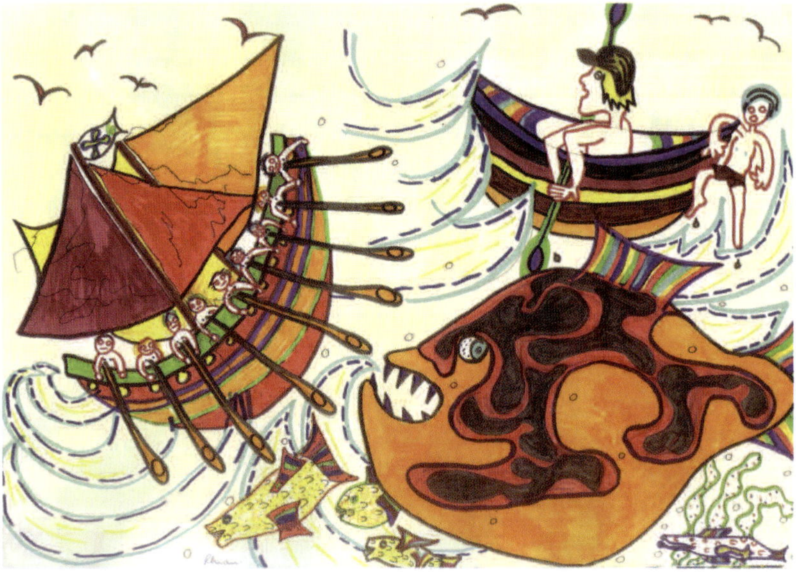

Rhian F. Miles

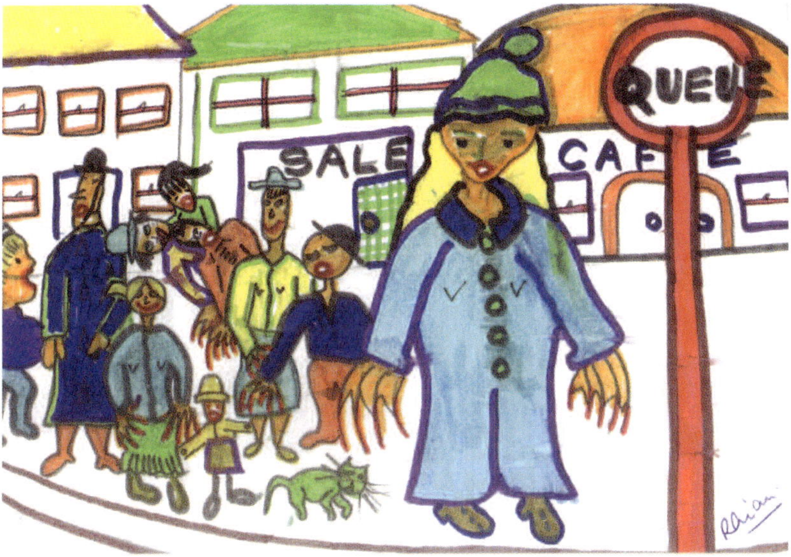

Rhian F. Miles

This piece of artwork expresses the theme of mind-space relating, as it does, to my experience of schizophrenia. I frequently suffer from visual hallucinations, the intensity of which is conjured up by the images used in this collage piece. Sometimes all I can see are these visions, which become my reality – my own internal world. These visions can make me feel extremely withdrawn and paranoid as I live within my own head.

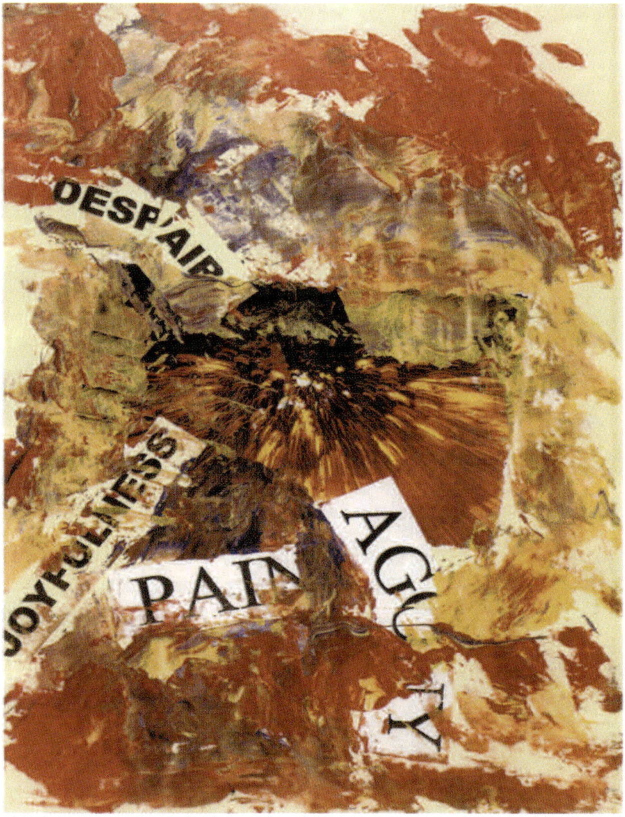

However, despite the negative experiences of my illness, I use my creativity to reference images of hallucinations, because by defining them I am in control of them. This allows me on one level to create more internal space within my own head. This acts as a means to connect a bond between my inward experiences and the external world.

Denise Searl

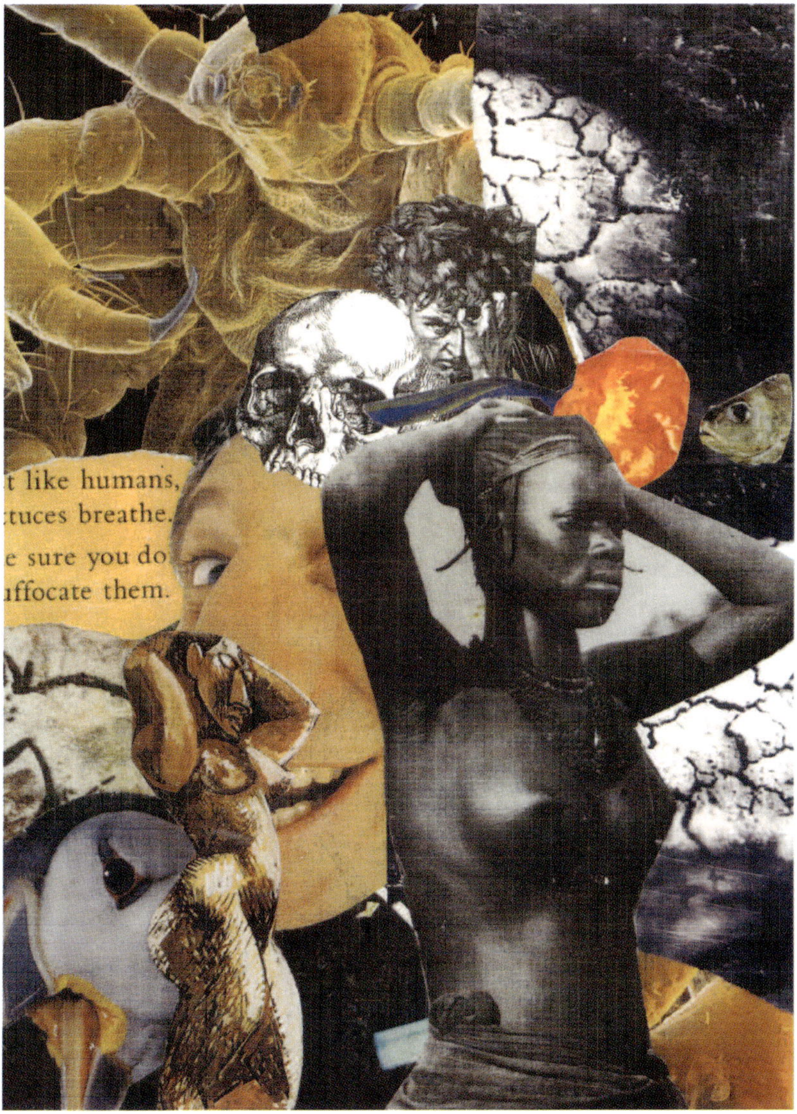

Denise Searl

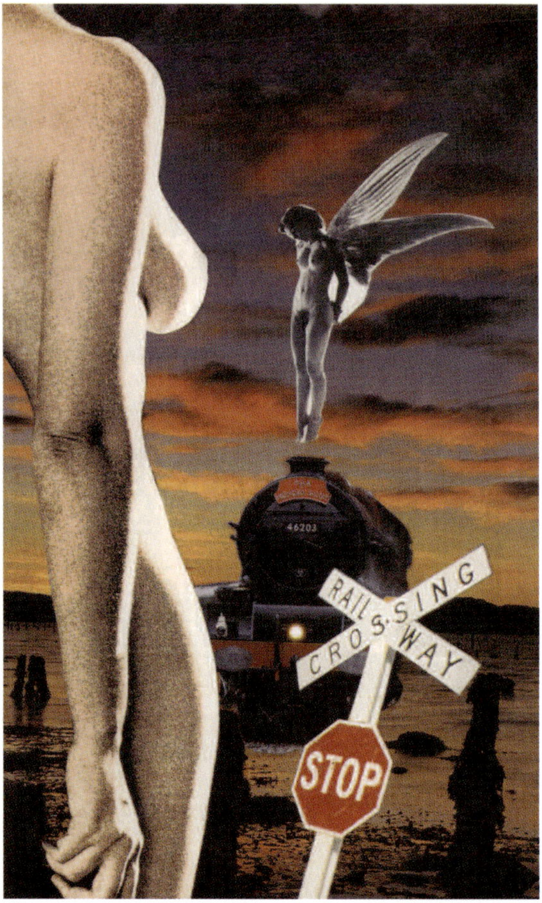

What dignity means to me... is a relationship with personal empowerment. The psychological dignity of an individual can be achieved through exploring intense, difficult and often extreme emotions in counselling and creative therapies. Unfortunately the mental health service does little to maintain this form of dignity. Most people who experience mental distress are labelled with a diagnosis and given powerful medication, which has unpleasant side effects. This does much to undermine an individual's physical and psychological dignity. To promote the dignity of an individual we need to understand that people are not just a collection of chemicals. We also have emotional needs and souls which we would be happy to explore through therapy.

Denise Searl

1970, then China also in 1970 and Britain the sixth to do so, in 1971. The seventh entity was Europe in 1979 with the launch of the first of the Ariane series of rockets, which have continued to be used for the launch of commercial satellites up to this day. The eighth, ninth and tenth were India (1980), Israel (1988) and Brazil (2004). I would welcome Iran into this space club, if it could succeed in launching a satellite into orbit. They are making the necessary preparations, having launched a rocket spacewards already.

I think it's a wonderful achievement for a country to launch a satellite into orbit. But even more wonderful to my mind is to launch a human into space. Manned spaceflight started on April 12, 1961, when the Russian Yuri Gagarin was lofted into space. America followed – again second, in this manned space race, as they were with a satellite launch – in May 1961 with Alan Shepard in a sub-orbital flight, merely touching space briefly. In February 1962, John Glenn was the first American to go into orbit. Then a long time afterwards, four decades in fact, in October 2003, China launched its own countryman, Yang Liwei, into space with home-grown rockets. China was only the third nation to achieve this. Astronauts and cosmonauts from many other countries have been in space, but only with the Russians or Americans, that is not launched by their own countries' rockets.

I would like to see Europe join this exclusive

manned space club. It has a craft, the ATV (Automated Transfer Vehicle), which has been tried and tested successfully in space, which could be adapted to carry European astronauts into orbit.

Outstanding in space annals is America's successful manned Moon landings in the late 1960s and early 1970s. Twelve American men have walked on the Moon during six lunar landing missions. China says it may land the first non-Americans on the Moon in about, maybe, 2020. We shall see.

Further, I would like to see British astronauts trained for spaceflight and go into space under our own flag, whether it be with the Europeans or the Americans.

In the news a while ago was India's launch of a Moon bound spacecraft, on October 22, 2008. India is the sixth country to send a spacecraft to the Moon. The first country was the Soviet Union in the late 1950s, then America, and Japan in 1990. Europe followed in 2003 and China only recently in October 2007, launching its Moon probe Chang'e 1.

Good luck to all these space-faring nations in their adventurous and thrilling undertakings. It is the stuff of dreams and along with it goes the achievement of national prestige for the countries that do so. As the Russian spaceflight theoretician Konstantin Tsiolkovsky said at the beginning of the twentieth century:

'The Earth is the cradle of Mankind, but we cannot live forever in a cradle.'

(Note: Iran succeeded in launching a satellite into orbit on February 3, 2009, after this article was written.)

An Evening at the Grosvener Hotel

Lenni Charles

Eileen sat back in the soft, plush armchair regarding Mel, and was pleased with what she saw. The younger woman was tall and sleek, with the kind of legs that went on forever. Her dark hair was cropped short, her skin tanned, and her large dark eyes gave her a Spanish or even Egyptian look.

'Well,' said Mel, urging her on.

'Oh yes,' said Eileen. 'You would have thought I'd have forgotten after all these years but it's still there as though it was yesterday. It was to be our big night out, at a grand hotel. It was a few days before Christmas and Kevin had been working as a night porter there for about a month; getting on quite well, very popular with the staff and customers. As a sort of Christmas treat he had arranged with the chief that we could have a room for the night, for a night of unbridled lust.'

I stepped out of the taxi and walked though the glass-panelled doors, into the entrance hall, all oak panels, brown desks and chandeliers. It wasn't as posh as the Hilton and some others that I had been to in my Aunty Beeb days but it had a kind of faded grandeur of bygone days. I stood looking around for a few minutes feeling excited and slightly guilty, with that deliciously daring feeling I used to get as a child when doing something a little bit naughty; then Kev came out looking quite flustered,

'The manager is still here... so I can't get you a key yet. Come into the lounge and have a drink while you wait, just look relaxed as if you are an ordinary guest.'

He led me into a large room lavishly decorated with flocked wallpaper, red paisley carpets and the ubiquitous chandeliers and ushered me into an armchair by a small table in the middle of the room. I would have been more comfortable at one of the side tables, but as it was only about nine o'clock there were plenty of people around so I didn't worry too much, and settled down with the very ample glass of brandy and Babycham that he set before me.

It was the beginning of a very long wait, alleviated only by either Kev or one of his colleagues turning up about every 30 minutes or so to replenish my drink either with the same or with whiskey and ginger;

always a large. Also, their behaviour was becoming more and more obsequious. On and on this went; if they expected me to pay for the drinks I would be in a difficult situation as I had only a few shillings on me, but they really couldn't as I had not ordered them in the first place. Still I was beginning to feel that things were not as they should be.

People began to leave. It was eleven o'clock. Now I was beginning to become quite uncomfortable. I was feeling both rather drunk and very conspicuous, in my chair in the middle of the huge lounge. The main chandelier was hanging over my head like the sword of Damocles. The clock went ticking on. The only people left in the lounge now were a large family group of Americans sitting at a table near the fire and a tall elderly gentleman dressed in tweeds and reading *The Times*.

I got up and went to the loo. When I sat down again my head started spinning. I felt ill. What was I doing here? Why had I come? I should go home to my parents' house but I had no money for a taxi. It was late at night, dark, and snow was falling outside. I was trapped in someone else's bad joke. My mind started going back over the events of the last year; leaving my nice safe job at the Royal Photographic with my own office and my own private secretary. Why? Because I was bored, dear boredom come back all is forgiven. I'd worked as a nanny for a while for Alma who was divorcing Strewen her pilot husband. So I ending up counselling them and they got back together, and there was no room for me. Then I got the bar job at the pub in Lambeth Walk. That was good; it was what I needed, hard work and plenty of responsibility to take my mind off the troubles of the past.

That was when I met Roy. He was a painter with the council, six foot tall with skin like deep brown velvet and eyes that you could fall into and drown. We talked and laughed together. It wasn't long before we became lovers. We made so many crazy plans; we were going to Paris together, together we were one. No one could hurt us. No one could make us sad. Life was perfect.

We had been together for three months when he suggested I go to meet his mum. Why did he have to do that? Why couldn't he have waited longer, maybe I could have dealt with it if he had waited a year or so! All the terrors of the business with Sam and the Africans came back. I couldn't deal with it. I couldn't go through all that again. So I ran; straight into the arms of Kevin Neville, forty-one, with a once handsome face run to seed. A loud mouthed scouser with a pint in one hand and a wad of betting slips in the other. Cold, cynical and just plain bad, I should have walked away. I would have if I'd felt whole enough to survive on my own. I would have today but you can't go back and rewrite the script. So anyway, there I was.

I was brought back from my reverie by the night porter, who was bending over me with a covered salver. We thought Madam might like a sandwich. The sandwich, when uncovered, was his piece de resistance. It was so covered with ruffles of tissue and garnishes as to be unrecognisable. It had not become fashionable at that time to place sparklers in celebratory dishes or I'm sure one would have been added. With much bowing and scraping he left the room. I was now quite sure that someone was taking the piss out of me. Finding that the thing itself was edible, prawn mayonnaise and cucumber in fact, and delicious, I ate with relish and the hope that a full stomach would stop my head from spinning. Then sat back, in a state of resigned curiosity, to see what would happen next. The dour pattern continued. I experimented by stopping drinking but the glasses only piled up embarrassingly. The clock ticked and time crawled on.

Finally Kevin came in and pressed a large key into my hand and helped me to my feet. To my astonishment the entire family of Americans stood and bowed me out. It's strange but in the flash of time the old family training came back to mind: 'Grace and serenity at all times.' With black murder in my heart, I smiled, gave the royal wave and left the room.

He more or less pushed me up the stairs, along several corridors and into a shabby room. Finding the bathroom, I and relieved my stomach of its torturous contents, then dragged myself onto the bed and collapsed.

'I've got something to do,' he said. 'I won't be long.'

'Fine,' I replied, already half asleep.

Sometime later I awoke to his shaking my shoulder.

'Wake up. I've been talking to the old guy with the newspaper and he's offered my twenty-five quid if you'll sleep with him.

'That's not funny,' I said, not sure whether I was still be teased.

'Aw, come on kid, we need the money.'

I wanted very much to slap his face really hard. I'm not sure whether I was too exhausted or had just become afraid of him. I simply burst into tears. He put his arms around me.

'There... there our kid... I love you even if no one else does,' he said, ever the master of the back handed compliment. I clung to him, for there was nothing else to cling to in that dark hour, and he made gentle love to me as I cried.

The woman looked up into the other woman's dark hazel eyes. 'I guess that was the night I conceived.' She sat back into chair.

'He always was a bastard, your father,' she remembered softly, but then with her head on the side and with a wistful smile, 'but he was never exactly boring.'

A Dialogue

Nyfed Griffiths

One weekend.

Jill: 'John, where are you?'
Pause.

John: 'What did you say?
I was in the bathroom.
I couldn't hear you.'
Jill: 'Oh, that's where you were.'
John: 'What do you want?'
Jill: 'I wanted to know where you were.'
John: 'I've told you.'
Jill: 'Yes, I know.'
John: 'Oh.'

John comes downstairs.
He plugs in the razor by the mirror and starts shaving.

Jill: ‘Do you have to shave downstairs?’
John: ‘What?
I couldn’t hear you. The shaver was going.’
Jill: ‘I said, “Do you have to shave downstairs?”’
John: ‘Why?’
Jill: ‘Why don’t you do it in the bathroom?’
John: ‘I have.
Oh, you mean shave.’
Jill: ‘Yes, what did you think I meant?’
John: ‘Oh, never mind.’
Jill: ‘But I do mind.’

John shaving again: ‘What?’
Jill: ‘Switch that shaver off while I’m talking to you.’
John above the sound of the shaver: ‘I can’t hear you. I’m shaving.’

Jill goes behind John and unplugs the razor.
Jill: ‘I said, “Switch that shaver off while I’m talking to you!”’
John: ‘But I haven’t finished yet.’

He plugs in the razor again and continues to shave.
Jill shouting: ‘John, you are the pink limit!’
John turns off the razor and says: ‘I heard you now.’
Jill exasperated: ‘When are you going to cut the hedge?’
John: ‘Oh, one of these days.’

Jill: 'You always say that.
Which one of these days?'
John: 'Oh, one of them.'
Jill: 'Which one?'
John: 'Well, I don't know if the hedge trimmer's working.'
Jill: 'Have you tried it?'
John: 'Yes, several times. Oh, you mean the hedge trimmer.'
Jill: 'What's the matter with you John?
Can't you concentrate for two seconds?'
John: 'Yes, I can, but I thought you wanted to know about the hedge trimmer.'
Jill: 'Oh saints preserve us.'
John tentatively: 'Saints?'
Jill: 'Oh, I give up. Why did I marry you?'
John soberly: 'Because you love me.'
Jill defeatingly: 'Yes, I did and I still do.'
John: 'There you are then.'
Jill cunningly: 'Do you think you could possibly try and cut the hedge, sometime this weekend?'
John: 'Let's have breakfast first.'
Jill: ' Oh, you're impossible.'
John: 'The difficult I can do now. The impossible takes a little longer.'
Jill despairingly: 'How long?'
John: 'Two days.'
Jill: 'Will you cut the hedge tomorrow?'

John: 'Let's have breakfast and I'll try the hedge trimmer afterwards to see if it works.'
Jill: 'Where is the hedge trimmer?'
John: 'In the garage, I think. But let's have breakfast.'
Jill: 'OK, OK. Truce for now, till we finish breakfast.'
John: 'What's for breakfast?'
Jill: 'Weetabix, milk, toast and tea.'
John: 'Is there honey?'
Jill: 'Yes, I'm here!'

Mind the Gap

Oskar Dremny

Wary of the gap, the old English gentleman stepped off the Circle Line train at the London terminal of the Great Royal Western Railway and walked up the stairs from the depths below: he had been underground for what seemed like an eternity and he no longer wished to reside in the dank halls underground and instead longed to walk on the surface of that most ancient city and take some fresh air. He was tall and thin with a proud posture and dark blue eyes that were quick and alert, combined with a nose that curved down towards his rather fat lips; his face bore the eagerness of a young man but combined with the guarded gaze of a much older man who was mindful that he was being watched. The uniform he wore was so old, tired and faded that the medals across his left breast more or less held the jacket together with their brass pins; they denoted a heroic act that he had committed long ago when he was a young man. An act that seemed like such a long time ago that sometimes he struggled to remember what had actually happened but he suspected that all men felt like that as some stage in their existence and he was no different from other men. Old but as yet undiminished, he limped onto the platform and rested for a moment whilst he surveyed the architecture with pleasure. The tall building was as he remembered it. 'Thank God,' he whispered to himself, thankful that his memories, if only when it came to architecture, were not diminished.

The designer ornate steel and iron archways of Brunel curved high into the air and across the platform just as they had done for the last 165 years. It was a marvellous piece of engineering. The GRW railway station had always made him proud to be British and he did so now, even when he was tired and old: so old that the trees had grown tall, so old that his bones were long since brittle and frail, so old that the shadows of the buildings around the station had grown disfigured, so old that he no longer spoke the language of London or recognised the many diverse languages that pounded its streets, so old that even he had almost forgotten how old he had become, and yet here in this special place whilst surrounded by the glint of Brunel's opulence, age seemed irrelevant for it seemed as if nothing had changed. When the station had first opened people had rushed to look at it, their eyes full of wonder and mouths filled with pretentious conversations about 'the magnificent timelessness of the architecture' and how such a design was a most suitable monument to the power of the British Empire; there could be no argument, it would remain unchanged forever. But if the architecture remained the same, everything else around it seemed to have changed.

The ancient thin man looked around him and suddenly he felt sad as he no longer recognised the populations, even though he was virtually surrounded by a quagmire of people: Polish students, Latvian backpackers, French men who looked like engineers for some reason, Russian businessmen who had just arrived from Moscow and were busy shouting into mobile phones about gas and oil prices. The shops and stores were full of Africans and Indians and there was even a shop staffed by yellow skinned people that had a small rotating menu with plates going round and round. But nowhere could he discern a local, someone with whom he hoped to start a conversation as he had not visited for a while and he longed to catch up with the latest news about the capital. But as he watched everyone rushed by with their eyes focused firmly on the pavement in front of them and there was nothing that he could do about it. A fat French man with wild hair and a dirty moustache rushed past in a ripped pair of jeans as he shouted some local French dialect into a cheap cracked mobile phone. The elderly man stared at him for a moment, reminded of his grandfather and his stories of the old enemy, but the wars with France had long since passed and in any case no one cared. He suddenly felt sad for all the young men who had died whilst fighting the wars against France and he wondered what they would say if they could see London now. For many years, he had felt sorry for the dead but now he was not so sure if they had not been the lucky ones.

At the station, no one paid him any attention. No one cared and it was as if he did not exist. A Polish man walked so close to the old soldier that he thought that he might walk straight through him without stopping, but the man turned to the voice of a woman at the last moment, his wife perhaps, who called to him with bagels in her hand. The tired man felt invisible and although the station was the same and it was exactly how he remembered it, the people who used it were entirely different and this was the aspect of his return that he found hardest to deal with.

The frail but resolute soldier looked up at the ceiling, searching for the architecture that made him feel at home. High up amongst the girders a small pigeon sat; it was grey and plump but still quite young, and it watched the hullabaloo of the station below with indifference. The soldier smiled as he understood the pigeon's reticence to get involved with the chaos below and he wished that he was young enough to climb up high into the roof amongst the girders so that he could sit with the pigeon. It would be nice to be able to touch the steel and iron girders that held so many memories for him. 'What fine stories those iron girders could tell,' he mused, 'if only I could sit and talk to them.'

He was sure people would think him mad for wanting to talk to an iron girder but he did not care for people these days. He didn't understand them any more. Still it was good to be back and he realised that he had left it far too long this time and that next time he should make sure that he visited London earlier. Sometimes he felt that he had so many places to attend to that his journey would never end. It must have been at least 35 years since his last visit.

He turned to face the hotel behind the station, but his left leg ached and was sore and as a consequence he limped. It was an old wound that he had sustained during intense fighting during the war: he had been in charge of guarding a regional headquarters, when a Boer counter attack had taken them all by surprise, enemy artillery shells thumping into the ground, sending huge plumes of earth into the air; soon the air was thick with dust, soot and deadly shrapnel. He had been hit early on and so was the headquarters set up in a local farmhouse, which had been hit directly by a shell that exploded in the second bedroom on the left side of the landing near a rather nice coffee table. Men and horses were stunned as the house had burst into flames, and all too soon, the ammunition that had been stored under the stairs, just in case of emergencies, exploded.

It killed everyone within a hundred yards.

The old man didn't want to remember the past; he made a deliberate attempt to stop thinking about it and instead limped towards the Great Royal Western Hotel, as he was unconsciously eager to surround himself in its uncompromising opulence. He had often fondly thought back to those wild and heady days he had spent whilst on leave in the hotel, as a young and vibrant soldier he had enjoyed every luxury that the British Empire could offer.

But he stopped as if puzzled. The hotel was no longer how he remembered it. It had changed, now it was called 'Hilton'. Externally, the hewn limestone hotel looked almost brand new, the limestone had been meticulously cleaned and the work had rid the building of 150 years of dirt and history that had clouded its image, but the once subtle décor of the opulent GRW Hotel had been replaced by garish signs of tack and bawdy. The old man reproached himself for being so superficial and decided not to let first impressions last. He decided to go closer for a better look and as he approached the steps, a group of beautiful women drew his attention; they were surrounded by old, wealthy but ugly men with big noses and odd shaped ears who smoked expensive cigars and whose bodies wavered under the influence of alcohol. There was talk of money in the air and it took him a while to realise what was happening; he had hoped to see the lavish hotel interior that he had once admired but he was so disconcerted by the realisation that the women were prostitutes selling their goods that he found it almost impossible to enter the hotel. He had long since relinquished the desires of the flesh but he looked closely because he had not seen a woman for a very long time and they reminded him of a lady he had known during a time when so many things that had happened so quickly. War did that, it made young men rush their lives and taught them to live for the day; he had been no different and by the time he had realised what he had, it had been too late.

The nearest girl wore a gold dress that clung to her every curve. On many women it would have looked beautiful but on this young thin wisp of girl, it looked clumsy, an idea that was confirmed by her ill at ease posture. To the old man who was a mere observer in this consumerist transaction, she looked tired and in need of a cup of tea. How he longed for a cup of tea; after all, that was why he was here.

He knew where to go. There was a small café nearby that made a splendid cup of tea. The wizened soldier winked at the hotel doorman, who didn't see him because he was too busy trying to remove the whores from the hotel steps without offending anyone, which was a rather delicate task. So the old lieutenant turned away and began to follow the street away from the hotel. The street continued long into the distance: red buses danced along the length of tarmac with dizzying speed, a red telephone box stood as a battered reminder of the past and there was an old sign high up on the brickwork opposite the hotel at the end of the terrace, which showed a faded picture of the railway that had long since ceased to exist. The terraced shops, on either side of the road, were topped by red-brick Georgian town houses that had been there forever or at least so long that it seemed that way. Even the grime etched onto the front of the houses looked tired: tired of standing on this street as time went by, tired of buses that passed without ever saying where they were going, tired of watching London as it constantly reinvented itself with every passing generation, and tired of being the same all these years later; not for them refurbishment or refinement at the hands of some skilled foreign worker, instead the grime was forgotten, impregnated, until it had almost become the houses themselves.

On the corner, opposite the telephone box, was the café. The café had at one time been called 'The Fallen Soldier'; it was called something else now but the old man didn't notice because his eyes were blurred and unfocused as the memories of the place swept him back into the past.

In his day, the tables had been covered in simple red and white tablecloths that glowed and dazzled with the light from the imperial blue London sky that blazed with confidence. Surrounding each of the tables were specially carved chairs that had been ordered from a talented carpenter based in Battersea Park and on the ceiling crystal chandeliers glistened and sparkled. Even the teapots were highly polished silver plate and the teaspoons were solid silver. The walls of the café were lined with solid oak panels cut from trees in the New Forest; the panels had been waxed smooth by years of careful polishing until the grain of the wood stood as testament to the strength of the country; capping the panels was a marvellously ornate cherry wood border that wound its way around the room, starting at the back of the café, passing round the tea urn and coffee pots where steam poured constantly towards the high raised ceilings, and then hugging the wall until it reached the motif.

The great painted motif, for which the café was justly famous, depicted the British Army fighting the Boer War, and it was a masterpiece that took up an entire wall of the café.

No one knew the name of the artist who painted the picture but there was no denying its impossible beauty; it was an exquisite painting of death. The Boer, that most anti-British of foe, had swept down from hills and surrounded the British Army, who were fighting for their lives. The Boers had German Mauser rifles, superior in range and accuracy, and had used them to good effect so that they had forced the British forces back to the lower ground. The British camp was in complete disarray: empty ammunition boxes littered the ground, dead British soldiers lay in a pile where they had been shot for cowardice by their own officers; horses and men who had been killed irrespective or rank or creed lay dead and scattered, and a few soldiers cowered behind their corpses whilst desperately trying to reload their guns. To the right of the picture, just above the first aid station, a cannon crew vainly tried to swivel their gun towards the onrushing Boer cavalry; the crew's struggle was brave but pointless as they were unaware that enemy soldiers crawled towards them silently through the knee-high grass, knifes in their mouths and death in their eyes. Enemy artillery shells thumped into the ground, sending huge plumes of earth into the air; soon the air was thick with dust, soot and deadly shrapnel. The headquarters had suffered a direct hit that had exploded in the second bedroom on the left side of the landing next to a rather ornate table; men and horses were stunned as the house burst into flames. It killed everyone within a hundred yards, including a young lieutenant with dark blues eyes. At the far edge of the picture, painted very small and almost missable if one was not paying attention, was the retreat of the British Army, and through the smoke of battle they could be seen burning and looting the farmships; shooting all the local men dead and then herding women and children away to the concentration camps.

It was here that the old man had come for his tea. The café has changed completely and was now a replica of millions of American cafés all around the world. The old soldier didn't note the details of this new café as he knew that they would not stand the test of time. Instead, he sat with stoicism and sorrow and looked at the great motif which was all that had survived time. He had forgotten so much since his last visit to this place; it disturbed him that he could have been so naïve at his age, and now that the motif was back in front of him, he suddenly remembered why he had left London the last time. It was too painful to sit here and relive all the memories: he missed his friends, he missed his love and his missed his era. He decided that he would just order a cup of tea and then be on his way.

The waitress was Polish and talked to her friend in a constant monologue whilst he found a seat. He didn't mind, he had time to waste, he knew that a young waitress would only ever see him when she was ready and not a moment before. She was far too busy talking to her friend to serve an old man like him.

Suddenly, a young man walked into the café. He was dressed in army fatigues and had a red beret folded neatly and tidily in his pocket. He was clean shaven and looked to be around twenty years old, although it was hard for the old war hero to tell. The younger soldier looked at the motif on the wall for a long time and then with a nod sat down opposite the old man.

'I heard you can get a good cup of tea here mate,' the young man said after some contemplation of the café around him; he didn't look overly impressed and why should he – after all the café had long since lost its grandeur.

'You could at one time... but not any more...,' the old man said, ruefully.

'Have you asked them?' the boy jerked his thumb at the Polish waitress.

'No point.' The old man shook his head.

'Why not?'

'Because those days are over... they don't sell tea here any more,' the old man said with a sigh and looked rather sad. 'Where have you come from?'

'Afghanistan... those days... what days... what do you mean?' the young man asked. Suddenly his eyes widened and in a moment of clarity and realisation he turned to look at the motif on the wall behind him; slowly and quietly... the old man simply disappeared.

The Martian Invasion

Nyfed Griffiths

We Martians are a warrior race. We tolerate no resistance. We have no mercy and we have little emotion as it makes us weak. Imposing our will gives us satisfaction. Resistance is futile. We sweep all before us.

We had entered the atmosphere of our neighbouring planet, Earth, and selected the westerly section of an island in the northern hemisphere, where it was daylight, to land. We saw a collection of buildings, including what we deduced were habitations, and found an open space. Some of the inhabitants we could see looking up as we came in to land.

They scattered as our flying saucer descended and touched down under power. The engines cut out and we looked out of our portholes. Most of the people had disappeared, but there were a few curious ones to be seen still watching our saucer. We waited and gradually two male persons came closer. Eventually the bigger one came up close to our craft and touched it. He received an electric shock and jumped backwards with surprise.

Our saucer is electrically charged after landing and slowly the charge leaks away into the ground. The bigger male turned and spoke to the other male, as the other male continued to look at the saucer. They couldn't see us inside because the material of the portholes only allows us to see out.

The other male now approached and he too touched the saucer. He only received a bit of a tingling feeling as most of the charge had leaked away.

The smaller of the two spoke to the other male, at which he, the other, looked incredulous. We gathered that the smaller male had told the other that he didn't receive much of a shock, but that the bigger male was disbelieving.

A young female came running up then, and before the other two could stop her she had touched the saucer with no ill effect. She called to others who were just coming out of hiding to come forward.

Soon, a small crowd had gathered and were examining our craft. We thought we would tolerate their curiosity for a while longer. We then opened the hatch and one of us stepped out. The crowd retreated when we opened the hatch. They seemed rather timid. We thought this would be a walkover. We had seen more aggressive and more timid races before.

We were taller than most of these Earthlings. Then we heard a wailing in the distance, and as it got closer we saw a vehicle come along a smooth surfaced stretch of ground. It had round parts, one at each corner, on which it travelled, and it was long and had a higher section in the centre with portholes, but they were not round, but roughly rectangular. There were another two males in this vehicle, which stopped, and they got out. The vehicle was white in colour, with black and yellow chequered squares on it.

The two came closer to our craft and one had a look of amazement on his face as he saw our crew member, who was taller than both of *them*. They were dressed in white on the upper body with dark blue clothing on their lower limbs. The one in front stopped and shouted at our crew member, who returned their gaze with a cold stare and said nothing. We did not understand their language and weren't interested in discussions, treaties or parley. It was they who would have to do our will or perish.

The second male from the vehicle held a small device and started speaking into it. The first male from the vehicle looked hard at our crew member. They were thinking what to do and it seemed had communicated with others like themselves or in command of them. It seemed these white and dark blue clothed persons represented some sort of authority. It meant little to us. No matter what authority they represented, we would overcome them. So far Earthlings had posed little threat to *our* authority.

Lilac

Rhian F. Miles

I like lilac in the spring, and the joy it
Brings to all,
Rhododendrons cast their spell after
Summer in the fall.
Violets pure and gentle, excel with lilac
Glows
And primrose shows its glory in the
Hedgerows where it grows.
Honeysuckle tall and mighty forms a guard
Above the hedge
And foxgloves form a mitten on each finger
Edge to edge.
Snowdrops in the gardens, grace their
Mantles to behold
And bluebells form a carpet, making
Footprints out of gold.
Pansies in the pots

Grace the cottage window,
And willow by the pond, embraces movement with
its billow.

But below there lies a threat, of
Encroaching mighty 'sods'
To destroy our ancient heritage, and to
Tamper with our 'pods'.

Guns, Tanks and Generals

Nyfed Griffiths

The 88 mm anti-tank gun, which was adopted from anti-aircraft work, was used with great effect by the Wehrmacht – the German armoured land forces – in World War Two. It could stop many an Allied tank dead in its tracks in North Africa and later in Europe, after the D-Day landings.

This millimetre rating refers to the bore or internal diameter of the barrel of the gun. An 88 mm gun fired compatible 88 mm shells – that is the shells were also 88 mm in diameter – and similarly a 75 mm gun would fire 75 mm shells. The shells were made for the particular gun.

It is said that Schindler's workers, whom he had rescued from the grip of the Germans, made shells to the wrong size so that they would be useless for the Germans. Indeed it seems that at night when no work went on in his factories, Schindler himself set the lathes which were to turn out the shells to the wrong settings. Schindler was a wealthy man who had strong Jewish sympathies.

On the Eastern front the German tanks met Soviet tanks with sloped armour at the front – the T34s. Many of the German shells fired at them would simply bounce off the sloped armour. So the Germans learnt a lesson, and adopted sloped armour for their very effective Panther tanks. This tank was armed with a 75 mm gun. The Wehrmacht eventually up-gunned their tanks, putting an 88 mm gun on another very successful German tank – the Tiger. It was a deadly weapon, although the Tiger's armour was thicker, and did not need to be sloped. The battle for superior gun power and superior armour continued throughout World War Two.

In response the Soviets up-gunned their T34s, putting 85 mm guns on their tanks and self-propelled guns. The self-propelled guns were vehicles with tank chassis and bodywork, but without the rotatable turrets which true tanks had. To traverse a gun on a tank, the turret had to turn, but with a self-propelled gun, the whole vehicle had to turn around. The advantage of the SPG was that it could carry a much heavier and more powerful gun. But it could be susceptible to attack from the side or from behind by an enemy tank.

In North Africa, I believe, the 76 mm gunned

Sherman tank with sloped frontal armour was first used by the British army, under a lend-lease agreement with America, which supplied us with tanks and aircraft during World War Two. However, the Sherman tank was a bit of a tinder box if hit by a German Tiger. It simply exploded in a fireball, more often than not killing the crew inside. The advantage of the Sherman was the vast numbers in which they were produced.

The Sherman tank was not very competitive compared with the German Panther and Tiger. However, by D-Day and the resulting invasion of mainland Europe, the British had had mounted their very successful 76 mm 17 pounder anti-tank gun on an adapted American Sherman chassis and called it the Sherman Firefly. This tank had comparable fire power to the German Panther and Tiger, against which it was quite effective.

The British also produced another medium tank, the Comet, with a slightly lower rated 17 pounder gun called the 77 mm, which was also quite effective against the Panthers and Tigers.

Towards the end of the war, the Americans produced the Pershing tank, named after the US General Pershing of pre-World War Two fame. The Pershing tank was armed with another anti-tank gun, the 90 mm gun, which was even more powerful and effective.

Many years ago I was enthusiastically building models of tanks and aircraft from plastic kits and have models of the Sherman, the Sherman Firefly, the Panther, the Tiger, the T34/76 and the T34/85 tanks as well as the anti-tank gun, the 88 mm one and half track tractor. It was quite a consuming hobby of mine.

Another US general, General Patton, who made great strides through Europe against the retreating Germans after D-Day and the Normandy landings, had a tank named after him, which came into service in the 1950s and 1960s. Although Patton was such a successful general, he was held back from taking Berlin, the German capital, before the Soviets arrived there, by Eisenhower, the commander of the Allied armies in Europe. Patton didn't like the Soviets and was ready to go to war against them, but there was collusion between the American and Soviet high commands and the American government didn't want Patton to upset the boat. Patton was such a firebrand that the American intelligence services clandestinely arranged for him to be killed in an 'accident'. Patton survived but was badly injured, and it seemed as if he was recovering fast, but the Soviets then played their part in finishing him off. George S. Patton will be remembered as a daring and flamboyant general.

The Germans had a good and charismatic leader of men too, in General Erwin Rommel, later to become Field Marshal. He was very successful in the North Africa campaign against us, until British Field Marshal Bernard Montgomery turned the tide with superior and determined forces and drove Rommel out of Africa.

Rommel went on to defend Fortress Europe against the Allies and was responsible for the formidable defences built on the Atlantic Coast. He was involved in the plot to kill Hitler and it is thought that when Hitler found out, he forced Rommel to commit suicide on the assurance that if he did so, his family would not suffer. I believe Hitler had a liking for this capable commander of his, but was disappointed by the involvement in the plot to kill the Führer, and offered Rommel this way out. So another good person met his end.

In the Soviet Union, General Georgi Zhukov was a brilliant and able military leader, instrumental in defeating the Germans at Stalingrad, and thus stopping their advance and driving them out of the Soviet Union. However, Marshal Josef Stalin, the head of the Soviet government, grew jealous of Zhukov and his success. The result was that Stalin duly demoted Zhukov after the war, but did not have him killed, possibly because Stalin thought he could have been useful had there been another military conflict.

Mysterious Journey

Alan Bowen

Whatever happened to the Manchester Piccadilly train on Wednesday evening on the 18th of March '09? Whilst travelling back on the same train from Wrexham to Cardiff Central I recalled a previous journey when a similar train arrived at the railway station of Abergavenny. At the station I noticed an electronic notice board which stated that the next train was destined for Carmarthen. I wondered at the time, being most surprised as to why the Carmarthen train was travelling behind the Cardiff train. I thought of getting off though I wondered if I was reading the notice rightly. I didn't have time to get off, so the train continued its journey. However, at my journey end I realised that I could have got off at Abergavenny and arrived back in Carmarthen about an hour earlier.

Guess what! Only just arrived home since leaving here

this morning, this is now Thursday, though I did come back for something to eat at lunchtime only to take my lunch to eat at the venue of a meeting; been out and about most of the time.

Did get to the library this morning, but I was only able to write some business e-mails which had to be written, then a friend of mine came along to talk when I was concentrating on what needed to be written. I intended to come back and write my letter to you, though as the afternoon meeting went on the time just went. When I arrived back at the library they were getting ready to close, they close at 5 p.m. on Thursday.

Excuse me as I eat some crisps, back to a routine of snacks, I wonder at times why I try so hard to keep things going, I need time for myself for a personal life, it took me quite a while to get to the library this morning, I spoke with people on the way, I jut find it difficult to get sorted in the morning these days.

I briefly called in at the café earlier on in the day, just to talk with someone I know; anyway I was trying to sort out about the group trip scheduled for next Tuesday. I sent a poster out. I was encouraged today when someone was delighted that the trip was going ahead and wanted a place on the bus. Later on in the day I was told that two more people wanted a place, though it seems that I will be in Cardiff again on the day in question. During the afternoon I was handed some more paper copies of the poster for distribution, so that people will know what to do, that is what day/time etc. for the trip.

For most of the day I have had a headache, but I am better now... I think, then worry... maybe I am struggling... though maybe not loving enough for myself for I miss out on meal times, I have doubts about why I am like this, then feeling tired, then the time has gone... what about holidays, all I know is that I do care, even if I am not all that good, I think about holding on then in my mind you close in on to me, to reassure you that I care about what is happening, then in my routine I get so entangled in daily routine.

Reality it is the present moment. I remember on the return train journey from North Wales that I happened to look out of the window to an information screen at the station of Abergavenny. The board gave details of the train that I was travelling on, then details of the second and third train. The second train was destined for Carmarthen which I thought was unusual at the time. I pondered then that I would catch the train further down the line, though somewhere along the line I lost the connection and was delayed at Swansea... sorry... I am rambling on again... what I am trying to say is that sometimes I get some sort of insight that I need to act on. The train journey yesterday comes to mind, for as I was approaching Abergavenny a thought came into my mind to try to look at the electronic notice board which gives details of the expected times of arrival of the trains. In fact looking back on the previous trip I knew that I should have got off the train to catch the Carmarthen train. If I remember rightly there was only a little delay, then I would have had a thorough journey to Carmarthen.

At Abergavenny yesterday, I was well placed to look at this particular notice board. There it stated that the next train to arrive was destined for Carmarthen, then the following train was destined for Milford Haven, which also had to pass through Carmarthen. I was too slow to react, so I decided to just keep on the train to the capital, that is Cardiff Central Station, then to catch the second train on the line to Carmarthen. When I got off the train at Cardiff, the notice board there stated that another train from London Paddington was to arrive first. That train was going to Swansea, so I decided to catch that train, it was the First Great Western train with first class accommodation, though I rather liked the ordinary trains for they have large tables. The train that had brought me from Wrexham to Cardiff Central was of the type which ran on the Carmarthen to Swansea line some years ago, so it was rather a sentimental journey as such... thinking that I had gone back in time, along the journey from Cardiff to Swansea, I noticed another information board. This time the Carmarthen train was the next one behind... though the Milford Haven train was not mentioned as far as I can remember. The train station at Cardiff had been very busy; when I arrived in Swansea I took my time getting out of the train for it wasn't going anywhere. To my surprise, there was another GWR train on the platform where I expected the Carmarthen train to arrive.

I will go back now to why I hesitated in getting off the train at Abergavenny. I had two sets of timetables on the table in front of me, neither of which gave details of the Carmarthen or Milford Haven trains, so that is why I stayed on the train. I was looking at the timetable when in fact I could have got off. Where was I... oh yes... I looked at the notice board in Swansea, no mention was made of the Carmarthen train, in fact the next few trains all terminated at Swansea. At this point all the trains had left the station, there was only myself standing on the platform. Except for a woman sat on the bench, the station was now deserted except for a train dispatcher with whom I went to speak. I was told that the Carmarthen train at this particular time didn't even come into the station, that it in fact bypassed Swansea. I asked about the Milford Haven train but I don't think he knew anything about that train.

So Carmarthen, a little town in West Wales, had priority in the evening over the city of Swansea. I had to wait about another hour or so on the cold platform at Swansea for a train destined for Carmarthen. To my surprise, the train was a GWR train; I didn't even know this type of train went to Carmarthen at this time of day. There were some other people in the carriage travelling westward, and when I eventually arrived Carmarthen after 10 p.m. there was a lot of activity. The railway station was in full swing, all brightly lit. I usually go out via the side entrance but to my surprise a new fence had been erected. On a Sunday, I usually just go for a walk down to the station; the railway station at Carmarthen is far busier than a Sunday at that time of night. Usually the trains are stored at the station overnight. I am puzzled by what is going on, it seems that the trains are now stored in Carmarthen, not Swansea. I have wondered about this before. Years ago trains used to travel northwards from Carmarthen. Though the links are very good it is when you have to go through Swansea that I seem to get stuck... something about the journey for my mind to read. I suppose if you were here this is what I would be talking about, I wonder sometimes if I am that person, that is I want to be, though in reality seem to be lacking in some way or other, only just turn round to look at the clock, it is 12.42 a.m. I better go to bed, I set up the laptop at the end of the bed. I have to stretch over to write... I am getting rather tired now... wanting to go to sleep.

My Favourite Book

Nyfed Griffiths

I'm so grateful to the late author Dr Paul Brunton for the spiritual guidance his book, *The Quest of the Overself*, gave me.

It is full of what I would call an uncommon common sense and the analysis section led me to beneficial meditations on the text.

I read the book at the right time in my life, when I was on a spiritual quest – seeking for something. It was destiny, I believe. There is a saying:

'When the student is ready, the master appears.'

This book, *The Quest of the Overself*, was the 'master' for me.

The book guides you through a series of meditations you have to do yourself, and encourages you to use your intuition – and I would say, experience – in a quest for an inner reality (which is the title of another of his books: *The Inner Reality*).

It is a quest for spiritual Truth with a capital 'T'. It is something which is knowable to all people, though many people may not use this book to discover it, and is the basis of all religions in my view. The yogis of old might call it – it sounds rather grand – 'a union with God' or as you might alternatively put it: a union with the Cosmic Reality or Cosmic Power.

The hippy might say: 'Peace, man, peace' or 'Love'. That doesn't mean that you have to take street-drugs to achieve peace, love and truth – you need to give love anyway and to receive it.

Truth, love and peace are part of the purpose of our lives. I may be preaching, but I know it's true.

Jesus, the greatest of God's messengers – to my mind – came to teach such a path of spiritual enlightenment, of spiritual truths. Yes, path. That is again almost the title of another of Dr Brunton's books: *The Secret Path*.

I found his books reassuring. Others might not. Although as I say he teaches in his book the truth behind all religions, it doesn't mean to say you need necessarily be without a religion.

In his *Quest of the Overself* book he mentions Jesus' words, called the Golden Rule, which is 'Do to others as you would have others do to you' – one of the best rules of life. Dr Brunton refers to different religions, different religious leaders and many sayings.

There is a teacher's saying I've heard of, which goes like this:

'What you hear – you forget;
What you see – you remember;
And what you do – you know.'

This quest is personal and you have to experience it for yourself to know it. It is not a second-hand experience.

Untitled

Alan Bowen

I keep six honest serving men
(They taught me all I knew)
Their names are What, Why and When
And How, Where and Who

Rudyard Kipling, *Just So Stories*

I had an uncle, one of my mother's brothers, contemporaneous with Kipling; as it happened he also had something else similar to this writer in that he spent some three years in India after the end of World War One.

India, that mysterious and exotic subcontinent whose ruby had been placed in the British Imperial Crown no less and one of whose female wearers was made Empress of India!

My uncle worked in British India and the India 'of the Raj': polo playing and gin and tonic under the parasol in the scorching sun. Away from all this he worked in a humble Colonial post office. A person of undoubted intellectual ability, he managed to gain an Army Scholarship to UCW Aberystwyth. Otherwise the sheer expense of entering a university would have been prohibitive – there were no benefits back then unlike today perhaps. He therefore managed to gain an honours degree courtesy of that august institution the British Army – specifically his regiment the South Wales Borderers based at Brecon. Unfortunately, despite being particularly fortunate in his military experiences (he had only the sole of one boot shot off by a sniper) he became a victim of the dreaded mosquito. Malaria then plagued him intermittently for the remaining years of his life.

Notwithstanding, he seized life with gusto, teaching in London, Cairo, Cork and Athlone in Ireland. His passion was tennis and cricket; naturally he preferred Indian cricket. Later, on medical advice he left teaching and ended up in Llangorwen Aberystwyth – 'the new Oxford movement' church – seat of Major General Lewis Pugh whose classic book *The Road to Endor* recounts the author's experience of escaping from a Turkish POW camp in World War One by speaking Welsh – the Turks thoughts he was a god.

Marrying late in life he still managed (or rather his wife did) to have two children and six grandchildren, then later two great grandchildren (to date).

He was regarded in high esteem by the family because although he was so far away, much further than today with the internet and 727 airbuses from Heathrow, rupees would periodically arrive for his mother living on the hill farm in a remote part of South Ceredigion near the northern Carmarthenshire border. I still retain the Post Office receipts for them.

A Tribute to Winston Churchill

Nyfed Griffiths

Leonard Spencer Winston Churchill, to give his full name, and his adventures were larger than life. I don't mean he exaggerated in his writings. On the contrary, he could see ahead; he could see further than the common man, or indeed could see further than many who were or thought they were better than the common man. But Winston had the common touch as well.

He was greater than many envisaged. One needs to read his words or a good biography about Churchill to appreciate him. It's something that many may not be able to see, or not be able to see immediately.

Winston Churchill was a man of immense stature. Without him, World War Two would very likely have taken a different path and we might be living under a Nazi regime right now. But reassuringly, this did not happen. Churchill was confident of a successful outcome to World War Two, in that Hitler would be defeated and we would be victorious. The fact that he was proved right is a testimony not only to his foresight but also to his contribution and commitment. Indeed, his foresight proved accurate on many an occasion in his life.

Churchill was many things. He fulfilled many a role. He was statesman, orator, historian, biographer, wit, war correspondent and brandy drinker. He was also less accomplished in the roles of artist, bricklayer, novelist, aviator, polo player, soldier and racehorse owner. Like the Renaissance figure Leonardo da Vinci, he was talented in many fields and in the annals of history he was a giant – like some Alexander, but of more recent times.

As Thomas Carlyle said, *'The history of the world is but the biography of great men'* and I would add great women too.

The Children Play War

Oskar Dremny

The two boys were at war. They had set up their game at home in the lounge as it was the biggest room in the house. In the corner of the room was a television that consistently showed the news channel; the sound of it filled the room, the images flickered across the screen with urgent need, bright lights flashed in the darkness as another missile landed in a far off land as a new conflict raged in the Middle East. And yet, the boys didn't pay any attention to the television; instead as children often do they focused with single minded determination upon the task at hand, which was to kill the army of the other with as much savagery and relish as they could muster.

For this war, just like any other war, there were rules: the Geneva Convention, the Human Rights Act, and for these boys a set of additional rules that had been imposed on them by a stern father who had grown tired of their ceaseless bickering; regulations that consisted of a single die combined with written and defined rules of engagement that were structured and fair but that ultimately would decide the fate of each army.

The rules had been designed to stop arguments; this type of laddish warfare often ended up in a fist-fight and on one occasion it had even required a trip to casualty due to the audacious use of a cricket bat. After the cricket incident, their father had become incredibly angry and outraged. After all he was a staunch liberal, and hence he had banned them from the ceaseless war and for days peace had come over the house. Armies had been grounded: troops, planes, ships and tanks all had stopped and there had been no more fighting, flying, sailing or sinking until their father had relented after weeks of silence on the matter. Unable to play their favourite game, the boys had stropped and moaned about the house for weeks until eventually and under much duress from his wife, the husband had hunched over the kitchen table with a paper and pen, and had drawn up the Rules of Engagement which he had then presented to his sons.

Of course the boys couldn't agree. And the rules had been argued over, rewritten, re-argued and re-written many times before at last they had been clarified, formulated and accepted. Even now, almost a year later, the system was being disputed by the younger of the two bothers, Mohammed, who still held a grievance against his older brother due to being hit by the cricket bat last year, and who strongly felt that those rules which in hindsight had been suggested by his older brother were not as unbiased as he had claimed at the time.

The older boy, whose name was Azzan, wanted to win. No, to state that he only wanted to win would be incorrect: it wasn't just the winning, although that was desirable, he wanted to annihilate his foe; there could be no peace, no respite until he had driven his brother Mohammed from the lounge forever. But for all of the older brother's determination to succeed and his skill with an army, his younger brother Mohammed was equal to the task and resolved to prove himself a worthy opponent.

Such was the detail with which they played that normally it would be a close game that could stretch out for many hours as the battles raged to and fro, until eventually someone cracked or made a desperate decision under pressure and the game would lurch towards an untimely end, or if the game had faltered and become drawn out then it would have been stopped for tea by mother, who saw no reason at all not to eat during a time of war. Food over, no quarter was expected or given during the battle itself and both brothers had developed unique and sneaky ways of inflicting damage upon the enemy forces.

The plastic soldiers had long ago been sorted into rank and regiment; many hours had been dedicated to painting the uniforms in the correct colour so that the battleground would look realistic. Tanks had been faithfully recreated, painted and adorned with the correct gauge guns, aircraft were selected by squadron and there was even a set of field artillery, enough for each side.

Traditionally, the loser of the last game was allowed to choose the new theatre of operations. This created great interest and debate as the boys researched history and decided which battle would be fought next. It was almost as much fun as fighting the game itself. Previously they had played World Wars One and Two and even once World War Three which admittedly had been rather hard to imagine and had involved the audacious use of laser beams, and of course there were the major skirmishes, the Vietnam war, the Falklands war, the Bosnian conflict; naval conflicts had not been ruled out either – Trafalgar and Jutland had always been firm favourites.

This battle was the choice of the younger brother who had lost the last war; he had lost as the British yesterday whilst re-fighting the Falklands war. It had been a painful humiliation and one that he resented enormously, so he was determined to make amends today.

The armies had been chosen and set up, which in itself could be a long winded process. But today for some reason both boys were eager to get started. So the game had begun. The younger of the two soldiers had deployed his troops so that they were protected by the terrain; on the right there was the sea that guarded the long strip of land which itself was surrounded on each side by the enemy. His troops were all camouflaged in civilian clothing and mixed in with the makeshift houses and rubble that combined to make a city; a toy city which stretched out across the rug for almost 3 metres. Fortunately, the younger boy had been planning for this war for a long time and for once he believed that he held a real unexpected advantage; although at this stage he was unprepared to reveal his secrets until the crucial moment of the battle.

His brother on the other hand was relaxed and calm. He had a massively superior force which consisted of tanks, aircraft, infantry and artillery. He had already begun his assault using aircraft and artillery and now he committed to land engagement using his tanks against the townships that stretched almost to the television. His aircraft had pummelled the ground for the last hour, making fast runs that started from the runway that had been set up on the kitchen work surface next to the defrosting chicken; a fact his mother disapproved off but did little to stop. It was harmless fun after all.

'I know what you're thinking,' said Azzan to Mohammed with a cocky grin that assumed he couldn't lose. He taunted Mohammed all the way through the game normally and now was no different, 'I know you want revenge for yesterday... but it wasn't that bad.... Argentina nearly won in real life... and this time... well this time... you're totally out gunned... you know you can't win, why not just surrender now and be done with it.'

Mohammed was not fooled, being well used to his brother's taunts. His forces had managed to halt the tanks from entering his city, albeit temporarily, and with the lucky throw of a six, his men had fallen back from the tanks without a single casualty, but whilst doing so had still managed to fire some rockets over the border towards Azzan's reserves.

'Well, I might get lucky this time,' said Mohammed with a wry smile. He had no intention of revealing his secret. He was desperate not to lose but equally resolved not to show his desperation to win, especially not to Azzan. More planes arrived from the kitchen and swept overhead, helped by the arm of his brother; they repeatedly attacked the town from the air, indiscriminately killing civilians and troops. In Mohammed's imagination he could picture the devastation. Azzan rolled a six and hit a school with his artillery; children were killed and lay dead on the street and the whole situation was rapidly becoming worse. Mohammed frowned at his lack of modern weaponry. He had no tanks, no aircraft and very limited anti-aircraft guns; hitting one of the fast moving jets was extremely unlikely and he was well aware that the airpower of his hated brother Azzan was killing his army. Mohammed switched his tactics and decided to scatter his men into the ruins of the town to try and prevent them being an easy target for the jets, but then he muttered a curse under his breath as he saw armoured helicopters coming from the kitchen.

The helicopters entered the lounge with a guttural whump whump noise that Azzan made by pressing his lips together and then forcing them backwards with disdain; the sound covered the lounge and filled Mohammed with dread for his men. He knew he was fast running out of options and decided that it was nearly time to use his own secrets weapon.

By this time the helicopters had left: they couldn't stay long as the rules dictated that the fuel load was defined by the dice, and for once Azzan had been unlucky and had rolled a one; hence the helicopters had turned back to refuel. But the damage of the helicopters had been ferocious; Mohammed's troops had been caught in the open just as they were dispersing for cover. It had been a massacre and a good part of his army now lay dead in the square at the centre of the city. Too late, Mohammed realised that should never had moved his men as one unit and instead should have spread them out completely. He knew that this battle was almost over but he would not go without a fight and the battle was not finished until his brother reached the square at the centre of the city; and besides he had something special planned. Assan fired off a few more rockets towards Mohammed's rear echelon which landed with a lot of fuss in a town area but achieved little if any military gain.

But time was against Mohammed. He watched with grim determination as Azzan began to reorganise his armour before the slopes of the city and then began the final push forward. It was time to act, Mohammed knew, but he hesitated slightly, concerned by what the consequences might be, but at that precise moment he looked at the television and saw clearly for the first time the images of yet another war strewn across its screen and with that in mind he resolved to continue the fight against his brother.

Yesterday during the morning, Mohammed had found his father's stash of fireworks in the garage; giant rockets that they saved for fireworks night and then sent flying into the sky. The local men of the village held a competition once a year to see who could send their rockets the furthest and each year his father would spend many evenings in the garage making his own rockets. Great excitement would precede the competition and every year his father would say that this was the year, but sadly his father had never won and bitterly resented his lack of achievement, as the other men teased him constantly about it. Mohammed sensed his father's disappointment even though he did not understand how to comfort him.

The rockets had been so well hidden from the prying eyes of young boys that Mohammed had almost not found them, and he had been close to giving up when he found a small tunnel in the floor that contained what he needed. With great patience, he waited until the middle of the night and then snuck outside and unassembled one of the rockets. It had taken him a long time; he had unscrewed the top, undone all of the pinning that held the rocket together and carefully worked his way down the rocket until finally he had emptied the device of its gunpowder. It was to be his finest moment in the war with his brother. He had no doubts that his brother would have no choice but to surrender on the spot.

Mohammed crept back into the house and removed the rug from the middle of the lounge; a rug that his mother has placed there long ago to prevent the children ruining the floor. He made a large deposit of gunpowder on the centre of the floor, a space where he hoped to lure the troops of his brother, and then he made a fine line of the powder towards the edge of the carpet where he knew he would be sat whilst the battle unfolded the next day. All it would take would be one small spark and the whole carpet would go up. Mohammed couldn't wait to see the shock on his brother's face when it all went up with a bang. It was going to be an awesome day. One long remembered.

And now Mohammed was here. In the moment that he had waited for all day for, his brother Azzan had moved his tanks forward once more and, backed by his infantry, they were cutting through the last of Mohammed's men with ease. It was now or never. Azzan had that confidant look on his face. He sneered at Mohammed, 'You have no chance little brother, I'm going to kill you again!' He laughed and moved one of his support vehicles closer to the front. Mohammed narrowed his eyes and looked at his own brother with hate, true undeniable hatred that could not be undone, and he whispered fiercely across the lounge to his enemy, 'You won't say that when I unleash my suicide bombers on you.'

Azzan snorted derisively, 'What are you talking about suicide bombers for... your army has no suicide bombers.' But even as he muttered the words, Azzan's eyes were drawn to his brother's fingers as if he was mesmerised; Mohammed held something unusual in them, something that instinctively Azzan knew shouldn't be there. A box of matches.

Azzan watched as Mohammed's fingers moved in slow motion. There was a glare as a small fire caught the end of a match and then it moved as Mohammed touched it to the floor. Flame raced under the mat towards the darkness at its centre. The explosion rocked the room. There was a scream and a rush of air as the window blew outwards in a rain made entirely of glass. Even Mohammed, who had been expecting it, was surprised by the intensity of the explosion. He was knocked off his feet by a big invisible hand and as he lay on his back stunned by the intensity of the explosion, the world took on a surreal moment, as Mohammed realised that his lounge now resembled the images on the television. His mother had rushed into the room from the kitchen and he presumed that she screamed although he could hear nothing. His eardrums had burst and he was deaf for life. Not that it mattered any more. He had been right. He had succeeded. His brother writhed in agony on the floor. His eyes were simply not there; they were burnt away. He was now blind for life. Mohammed watched as his mother ran this way and that. Eventually it was all too much for her and she fainted. Peace settled over the house for just a few seconds and Mohammed smiled serenely and leant against the sofa. In the corner unperturbed by all the noise, the television still continued to run the news and Mohammed began to watch it despite the glorious silence in his ears; after all it was his favourite show.

Untitled Story

Rhian F. Miles

Whatever happened to cosy evenings, sat around the only fire in the house; when Mam would gather our nightwear and prepare us for bed. Then at the given moment, the marching orders were given, and all three of us children would brace ourselves to the the cold and run like our little lives depended on it up to our beds. The bedrooms were freezing and our mattresses made out of bristly old horse hair, with three bulky old eiderdowns gracing our beds, in the hope of capturing some heat. We all had (thanks to Mam) china hot water bottles, which although bulky, were magic for warming up feet – to hell with the chilblains. The three of us huddled up in the single bed, oblivious of life's problems, but soon, the wise ones decided Robert would be best suited in his own bedroom... that left my sister and me alone. We used to draw figures and shapes on each other's backs in the dark and in turn would guess the picture – what fun we had, full of raucous laughter, until one night our disturbed father (in the next room) caused untold damage and smacked my bare bum until it was raw. The next night we had separate rooms! Whatever happened to family life now in 2009... some say progress!

Jesus

Nyfed Griffiths

In the end, they killed him, because they didn't like what he said and did.

This man was a son of a carpenter. He had ideas above his station, some thought.

He was a revolutionary. He had ideas ahead of his time. It takes somebody like him to introduce such ideas. The ordinary, broad-minded, open people welcomed him.

He made waves and they reached the people who didn't like what he said. To them, he taught alien ideas, but they were the aliens.

His ideas made such a great impression. He turned the Old Testament on its head, though he said: 'I come not to destroy, but to fulfil.' He was a man of true vision and dynamism and compassion and love.

He could see what other people failed to see. He could see the potential in individuals. I'm pretty sure he never really gave up until the end, when he said, while dying on the cross, 'My God, why have you forsaken me?'

But two thousand years later, we can testify that his was the victory, with a system of belief based upon his teaching still surviving.

Off the Rails

Rhian F. Miles

Platform 3 in Swansea railway station was full, as usual, as commuters coming from work were winding their weary way home. The passengers were tired – it had been a long and arduous day for most and amidst the crowd, there was Dafydd.

Dafydd knew the route off by heart; after all he had worked with Swansea Council for nearing 25 years, and knew most of the 'regulars' on board. He did not converse a lot although he was an educated man, and preferred to keep his thoughts to himself. Most of his family and friends were very wealthy people, and would not dream of travelling on a train, when they had modern motorcars and private jets at their disposal – but Dafydd was a 'thoroughly modern Millie' and preferred the regular daily trip by rail.

In his youth, Dafydd used to work as a labourer on a nearby farm to get some well-earned money, which he saved and spent on a miniature railway. Some of his cash, which he endeavoured to put aside, would be spent on magazines about trains and engines; and he was well versed in the workings and maintenance of them. Even today, when he had time off from the council (evenings and weekends) he would still volunteer his services to toil the land with his friend farmer Bill – and in return he would receive a hearty free meal and a pint of free 'brew' or two from the barrel at the farm. Dafydd did not have to worry about the drink and drive law, as sometimes he was only too happy to take a stroll home, or as his house was on farmer Bill's private land, he was exempt from the law. He often chuckled at his fortune and others' misfortune, that there was always a way around the commons man's law.

Dafydd appeared to one and all as a simple man of few needs, and related to the every day person. He enjoyed his council job and his off duty work, but hidden amidst this façade was a very different man. He had always held desires to be a wealthy country landowner, and once his labouring job was over, he would want for nothing!

He practised on his miniature railway signal box to redirect the oncoming trains into a siding; where they would come to an abrupt stop at a dead end. This he practised daily, and one day Dafydd thought he had got it off to a fine art and felt his get rich quick plan was ready to be implemented. He had followed the routine of the mail van, which ran every evening from platform 3 of the station; also on that train from London, was the gold bullion Securicor cargo. This train would pull out of Swansea on the dot every night, and there were no armed guards to protect the cargo, only an engine driver and a ticket collector. Dafydd decided to follow his plan A of being a highway robber who would be rich forever.

He had made exploding bombs from common fertilisers, hydrogen peroxide, and 3-inch nails, which he wrapped carefully in his old socks. He embarked on the train. The platform guard blew the whistle, all of the carriage doors were then closed and exactly on time the train pulled out of platform 3. Once it picked up speed, Dafydd decided to use plan B and to throw very small incendiary bombs (like party poppers) out of the carriage windows. Upon hearing these explosions the ticket collector pulled the emergency cord, bringing the train to a halt.

Dafydd entered the engine room where the driver was, and demanded he strip naked from his clothes; if he did not obey Dafydd's orders, he would be forced off the train with a sock in his mouth. In minutes, the ticket collector arrived on the scene and he too was ordered to strip naked and remain in the engine room. Dafydd removed the ticket collector's money bag and whistle, rendering him helpless, and tied them both up with rope, so there was no escape. He also tied some of his homemade bombs to their heads, with the ominous flex hanging from them, which could be lit should the rail men attempt to use the alarm.

Dafydd took charge of the train engine and directed it to a siding, where he had already prepared a hydrogen balloon and its basket. He pulled the engine up, and loaded the gold bullion and Royal Mail cheques, giros and postal orders. When all the work was done, he threw all the train driver's and ticket collector's clothing out of the window, setting the train to continue its journey, where they (hopefully) would return safe in the far distance, but should they squeal, then there was detonator on their heads, which would blow them all to kingdom come.

Meanwhile, Dafydd set forth in his hydrogen balloon (complete with gold and money orders), flying higher and higher until he was above the clouds and could no longer be seen by the naked eye, only leaving a vapour trail behind him. And he was never to be seen again.

Cheryl

Oskar Dremny

The hut where I had chosen to end my days was hidden in the mountains, far away from the prying eyes that were looking for me. I had travelled far and was weary with sleep deprivation and I stumbled along until I turned left at the old walkway through the forest: walked past the thick gauze brush-like plants which stuck to the legs of my trousers, then strode along the damp rocky bed of a stream, thereby soaking my boots, a stream that would become a raging torrent of froth and spray in the first melt of the spring; yet still I did not stop walking until I crossed the small frozen lake on which the hut was a resident.

The oak timbered hut sat, tiny and small, in the foreground of a huge range of mountains, a panorama in which the hut looked overwhelmed and minuscule, but I knew that it contained everything that I needed for life. I did not need the trapping of a happy life. I just needed to exist, at least for a while until I had re-gathered my strength. I had known for some time that I would end up here, as that was the type of character that I was, full of self awareness but with self loathing and a destructive streak that followed me everywhere.

After a few busy days, I had settled into the hut, the cobwebs were swept clean, the rats slung out, albeit temporarily, and my dog Trevor and I were sat in front of a warm fire. Not a moment too soon, as the clouds began to darken and the smell of snow was in the air. That night as I lay in my bed my heart ached with the pain that only one who loves with freedom can understand. She had left me. I didn't know why. But that was the truth. There was no consolation, no understanding or acceptance, and I wept as the snow flakes began to silently fall to the ground.

It was the hardest winter I can remember. Even the trees, lanced by shards of ice, seemed to shudder in the harshest of morning sunlight that burst across the mountain behind the house. An avalanche fell on the cabin last night and now I was trapped in desolation by the very climate within which I sought refuge. Trevor and I would have to try and dig ourselves out when the daylight appeared through the snow.

Even though there was nothing to do, I could not sleep as the memories of her kept me awake. Like the cold itself they had a life of their own. I could not control them any more than I could control the fierce winter that had stripped the cabin of all its warmth.

Many weeks later, but still trapped by the devastating winter chill, I had awoken early, tired after the long hours of darkness. The icy wind howled through the eaves, as snow flakes blew in via the gap in the old jagged door and then committed suicide in the oblivion – like warmth of the roaring fire.

Despite the fire, the condensation had frozen on the inside of the window and for once I did not waste any energy chipping the brittle life source from its make – shift picture frame that spoke of a world outside.

The picture frame had a unique perspective: snow, white snow, grey snow, black snow, half melted sleet, cold slush, indifferent, inhuman, and lifeless; it was all piled up against the outside of the window like the story of a thousand winters entwined with my own despair.

How many weeks had it been since the cabin had last seen sunlight? I knew not. I did not know if humanity could live without sunlight, but I had discovered that I could not.

My rifle rested against the frozen inside-wall of the cabin. The condensation had run down the barrel and had frozen the firing action internally. It had been my final solution to the problem and now even that last despair had been taken from me. Perhaps, if I am lucky I will freeze quickly rather than starve, as I cannot remember when last my tongue tasted anything but diluted snow.

The food was finished last week. I gave the last of it to Trevor my dog. Yesterday, he sloped out of the door with his tail between his legs and left me; I think in the end that he could not stay to watch his master die.

If Trevor had lived, and the snow and the terrible ice would just untie my legs that were frozen to the bed, then maybe, just maybe, I could have escaped from this end of my own making.

My skin is blistered, burnt and burst from the burning touch of the steel bed frame, and the blood that used to pump around my feet has stilled as skin and flesh turned to solid, cold, ice.

As the ice creeps higher up my body, I welcome its touch as it stops the pain in my heart. She, her, that woman that I loved, did not want me and now as my blood runs cold, even colder now as the wood is run out and the fire diminished, at last I will know how it feels to be her: cold, calculating and indifferent; the terrible queen of winter that turned my world to ice.

Forever, I will be like her: frozen and cold. Now that the ice burns it ways up my leg, and into my heart, I know there is no resolution or meaning.

I am desolate like the ice that surrounds me, terrible like the snow that buries me, and my soul is filled with vacant despair. Truly, I am as cold in desolation and isolation as I was warm in love. Now that I am her match, perhaps she will love me and have me back.

From somewhere outside in the desolation, I hear a sound.

'Jack!'

A deathly silence surrounds the hut.

'Jack!'

Silence.

'Jack!'

'Yes mum! I'm busy! What is it?'

'Its tea time... and it's getting cold. Are you in the airing cupboard again?'

'No mum!'

'You bloody well better not be, I need to hang my best towels in there to dry. Aunty Sharon is coming over for wine and biscuits.'

'I'm not in the cupboard!'

'Good.... Oh... and Cheryl rang. Now what was it she said? Oh yeah. She said she was sorry.'

'Sorry? Just sorry! Is that all?'

'Yeah and... err... she still loves you.'

Suddenly the chill was gone and Jack felt unbearably warm.

'I'll be down in a minute!'

Jack opened the door and left the hut that had been his sanctuary for nearly the whole afternoon. He blinked in the bright sunlight, and then shut the door to his hut of despair and went downstairs for tea.

A Favourite Place

Nyfed Griffiths

This is a favourite place of mine. It is my home. It is a white detached three-bedroom house located in the well-off area of my village, but the outside walls need a coat of paint. It's almost twelve years since it was painted and it'll cost a few thousand to paint, I reckon.

On the apex of the roof there is now only one chimney. The other has been removed. Both chimneys were leaking and the removal of one of them – unwanted – and the insertion of a lead tray in the other has fixed the leaks, thank God. That cost a few thousand pounds too.

This place, my home, holds hundreds of books and I've taken measures to store most of them – or rather, display them on shelves – a while ago. I have a six-shelved bookcase holding books on space, reference, World War Two, Observer's Guides, *Sunday Times* special supplement files and magazine holders.

Apart from books, there are many pictures hanging from the picture rail in the same room as the large bookcase, already mentioned. This room is the lounge, situated at the front of the house, by the main road and facing south-east. This room has a bay window.

In the lounge, one of my favourite rooms in the house, there is also an item of furniture, holding in excess of 100 audio tapes on racks.

There is also a display cabinet; one of its sections has smoked glass doors with glass shelves inside, holding antique china and glassware. Beneath this display cupboard section of the cabinet are LP records and more books. Beneath *these* are drawers containing photograph albums and old greeting and sympathy cards, from when my mother died, which are of sentimental value.

The rest of the display cabinet houses some paperbacks, hardback books and family photographs. Beneath these shelves is a space holding a record player and boxes of more audio tapes and some single records. Beneath *this* are more and deeper shelves holding large coffee table type books and 'The War Papers' files – facsimile copies of World War Two newspapers and *The Times* ancient and medieval history files.

On top of this display cabinet are other favourite things: three Corgi models of various Mansel Davies lorries – a local company; four Weetabix lorry models; and commemorative plates and antique glassware. I was lucky enough to buy this display cabinet, whole and undamaged, for about a tenner in an auction.

I also have a very comfortable three-piece suite, bought after the house was renovated twelve years ago. The large bookcase is a more recent acquisition along with a shelving unit, which is much narrower than the bookcase and almost as tall at around six foot. The shelving unit holds some interesting large and small books, stationery and photographs, which have not been put into albums, as well as some box files on the bottom shelf. I assembled the shelving unit myself from a flat pack, bought from the new Focus store in the local town.

There is also a mantlepiece over a covered fireplace, holding china dogs, more commemorative plates, family photographs, a specially made mug with my name on it, given to me by a now late, close friend. And a favourite birthday card depicting a teddy bear removing a DIY book from a high shelf.

There is a table in front of the fireplace, holding an old panoramic secondary school photograph of all the pupils and staff of Ysgol y Preseli in 1959; my mother's teddy bear – that is, a cuddly toy; a stand holding CDs and a CD player. Below the table are an orrery in its box, a wooden Noah's Ark and animals I made using a fretsaw in occupational therapy while in a psychiatric ward, a ghetto blaster and a portable black and white television.

I'm going to describe one other set of things. They are postcards stuck onto the display cabinet by Blu-Tack. One shows a mountain with a man sitting on a rock. To me this means a spiritual quest for fulfilment and maybe further chances to preach sermons. Then there is a postcard of a bride outside a chapel, which shows my wish to get married one day. Thirdly, there is a *Reader's Digest* postcard showing piles of cash in the boot of a posh car. This shows my wish to possess a substantial amount of money, so I can do what I want and be secure financially.

Acknowledgements

This book has come about largely through the involvement of ArtsCare/GofalCelf tutors Damian George, Carole Morgan Hopkin, Moyrah Gall, Sue Holingsworth and John Weston. A large contribution has also been made by Angie Darlington and Jill Jones of West Wales Action for Mental Health.